Guide to
Legal Writing Style

Guide to
Legal Writing Style

Terri LeClercq

Senior Lecturer
University of Texas School of Law

Little, Brown and Company
Boston   New York   Toronto   London

Library of Congress Catalog No. 95-76102

ISBN 0-316-16302-3

CCP

Published simultaneously in Canada
by Little, Brown & Company (Canada) Limited

Printed in the United States of America

IN MEMORIAM

RAY COOK

Ray Cook, a colleague from the English Department and School of Law, University of Texas, was killed by a drunken motorist after teaching only one year at the law school. Ray encouraged me to join the faculty at the Law School, introduced me to books on legal writing, and encouraged me to develop an exercise-based writing text that would help future law students.

Summary of Contents

Table of Contents

Table of Contents

Preface

It is a compliment to be told you think like a lawyer, but an insult to be told you write like one.

Legal writing is a technical dialect. Although it shares many characteristics of nonlegal writing, it can nevertheless be mystifyingly different to new legal readers and writers. This book investigates the unique and sometimes peculiar style of legal writing so that you can create, and edit, a professional legal style that avoids the pitfalls of legal dialect.

How This Book Works

In the first stage of writing, most writers necessarily concentrate on the "what" rather than the "how" of their message. But even the best writers sometimes forget that the "what" is only as effective as the "how." This book is intended to help writers move from a substantive first draft to a polished final document.

Developing a professional legal style is more than mastering grammar and punctuation rules. To select words and sentence constructions is to take advantage of available options. Good grammar is not an option. Sophisticated and deliberate style is. The English language fortunately contains a wide variety of stylistic options from which a competent writer can choose: options in word choice, sentence structure, punctuation, and organization. The book introduces you to many of those options so that you can create powerful, professional prose that still reflects you and your writing goals.

Most careful writers begin the second stage of writing by reviewing their raw draft material. During this stage, they determine what information is essential to their readers and reorganize their draft material to provide the necessary information in a suitable format. Chapter 1 focuses on the deliberate organizational choices you can make that will allow readers the most effective access to your material.

Once the main ideas are reorganized and highlighted, careful legal writers edit their drafts a second time, concentrating on the clarity of each sentence. At this stage, they refine sentence structures so that each sentence offers a crisp and succinct message, a craft that Chapter 2 will help you hone.

Word choice is crucial for style, and Chapter 3 explores options available for word choice—words with obscure or highly specialized meanings, words that destroy credibility, and words that change a sentence's meaning if they are misplaced.

Finally, Chapter 4 explores the stylistic options of punctuation and contrasts them to the rules of punctuation that are not optional.

Within each chapter are short exercises designed to reinforce the specific stylistic device discussed. Additional exercises at the end of each chapter allow a separate review of those editing methods.

The book also provides a practical Appendix that includes reviews of essential grammar and punctuation rules, plus examples of a student-written memorandum and a brief, along with writing instructors' annotations.

How to Make This Book Work for You

Before your first written assignment, you may find it helpful to skim this book so that you can acquaint yourself with what is expected of legal discourse. Then after receiving an assignment and completing a first draft, check it against Chapter 1's suggestions for organizational cues. Next, fine-tune your sentences by comparing them to Chapter 2's suggestions. Evaluate your word choice using advice from Chapter 3, and finally review punctuation strategy described in Chapter 4. After reviewing each step of your style, you're ready to turn in your final draft.

When your paper is returned, focus your efforts on the instructor's feedback by turning back to the chapters that address your weaker areas: We all have some glitch that can be smoothed over for a rewrite or practice edit. For example, if your instructor had trouble following your analysis, you might want to review the organizational exercises at the end of Chapter 1 to see if clearer transitions, headings, and cues will help highlight your improved organizational scheme. If your sentences were too complicated or your word choice awkward, practice the exercises within each subsection and chapter conclusion to Chapter 2 or 3.

All law students and new attorneys share a certain degree of anxiety about legal writing, and for good reason. Your new audience is demanding and expects logical reasoning and precise presentation. Why? When you are practicing law, there will always be an opposing lawyer paid specifically to scrutinize your writing and find weaknesses in your argument and ambiguity in your prose. The opposing lawyer will capitalize on them. That opposing lawyer should always be part of your intended audience as you write.

This book cannot answer all your questions or calm all your anxieties about writing, but, by using this book, you can develop into a careful writer now so you won't be vulnerable later.

Acknowledgments

Many colleagues and students have encouraged me during the rough draft process: My special editor, Fred Asnes, read each version of the manuscript and provided invaluable support; two directors of the Legal Writing Program for the University of Texas—Susan Heinzelman and Christy McCrary—made suggestions for each chapter; the 1984-1994 teaching quizmasters and research assistants evaluated the manuscript; and the 550 new University of Texas writing students encouraged me, each year, to use their examples so that others might learn.

Guide to
Legal Writing Style

CHAPTER 1

Organizing with Style

I don't care how it's organized as long as it makes chronological or neurological sense.
—*Comment from a clerk who was reading a stack of briefs*

This chapter focuses not on how to organize and how to create a draft but rather on how to *reorganize* and how to *craft* the results into a final product once a writer has tentatively chosen the content. In the stage beyond the first draft, writers thus shift from *what* they are saying to *how* they are saying it and *to whom*.

Organization on the macro (overall) level includes a general introduction, the ordering and cohesion of major parts of the whole, and a conclusion. Organization on the micro (paragraph) level refers to paragraph development and internal cohesion. This chapter focuses on techniques for highlighting both levels of organization so that readers can easily understand, by skimming only the introduction or by rapidly turning the pages, what the document is about and how the parts fit together.

Analyzing the Audience

There is no static answer to any question of organization except that the writer's choice of organization should meet the audience's needs. An initial letter to a client, for instance, will be organized one way for a client with a legal background but probably another way for nonlegal clients. The layman may expect the answer up front followed by suggestions for further legal action. The legal audience may first need to review the legal reasoning before moving into suggestions for the future.

A final document follows the commonsense rules of audience awareness:

- Decide what information the audience expects.
- Place that information up front.
- Anticipate organization with a set-up that answers your readers' questions.
- Conclude with a summary or offer to provide additional information.

Post-Outlining Your Initial Draft

To determine what information you have placed—and where—in your draft, jot one sentence or phrase in the margin of each paragraph that summarizes the paragraph's purpose. Then quickly read through the notations, checking to see if they follow a logical order. If not, you can rearrange. If they do, then make sure that they are logical not only for your purposes but also for your audience.

This marginalia technique is also a good way to identify problems with transitions. If one idea in the margin seems to have no connection to the next, then double-check the paragraphs' conclusions and introductions for connectors.

Using Introductions, Set-Ups, Theses, and Road Maps

If the marginalia review of your document's organization reveals buried information, the easiest cure is a new, deliberately crafted introductory paragraph that should include the necessary procedural context, a "set-up" containing a thesis statement (and perhaps conclusion), and a "road map" if the material is divided into sections. This sort of internal cueing follows the adage, "Tell them what you are going to say, say it, and then tell them what you have said." This didactic style allows readers to feel comfortable with what follows; a comfortable reader is a grateful reader.

The introductory *set-up* paragraph explains the overall issue and some sense of the conclusion. It is a textual outline of the information to follow, indicating the relative weight of the parts and the order in which they will be discussed. If the document has several legal points, each needs a section that contains a small-scale version of the introductory set-up.

Thesis statements vary by function: The thesis of a memorandum, for example, is predictive, leading the reader from the legal issue to a short, general conclusion that precedes a balanced analysis of all pertinent theories and cases. The thesis of a brief is persuasive rather than predictive, and thus argues a conclusion that the brief will afterwards support through cases and theory. Statements of fact rarely begin with a thesis but can, especially if the facts are organized around a specific principle other than chronology.

A *road map* foreshadows the organizational pattern to follow. It might be a quick overview of the three exceptions to a general rule. Like a real road map, it can explain how long the traveler will be on the road, where the most interesting sites will be found, and the major road divisions along the way.

Look at the following examples from different legal documents and examine the introduction, the set-up, and the road maps for these different formats and audiences.

A memorandum:

The present lawsuit concerns the Plaintiff's attempt to set aside the Compromise Agreement. When the court examines the facts, the attempt should fail. As you know, a Compromise Settlement Agreement (CSA), which is approved by the Industrial Accident Board, is determinative of compensation to which the injured employee shall be entitled; however, if procured by improper means (fraud or mistake), it may be set aside by a court judgment and the case remanded to the jurisdiction of the Board for further rulings on the original claim.

Generally, a party seeking to set aside a CSA may do so based on equitable grounds of fraud. The party must show, among other things, the following: false representation by the carrier or employer (or their agents); reliance on the representations in making the settlement; and existence of a meritorious claim for more compensation than has been paid.

In a suit to set aside a CSA, the individual facts of the case are critical. The courts will look closely at the factual situation to determine whether the elements listed above are present. The following is a discussion of the facts in our case as compared to pertinent case law.

A law review note:

This note will explore the validity and value of the two solutions to redlining. The first issue to be examined is what federal regulatory measures exist to prevent insurance redlining. This discussion will encompass the history of the anti-redlining provision within the 1988 Fair Housing Amendments (FHA) Act, the HUD regulations enacting the 1988 FHA Act, and whether these regulations can withstand judicial review. Second, the Texas Insurance Code and Deceptive

Trade Practices Act will illustrate the inadequacies of available state solutions.

Using Headings as Signposts

In addition to adding introductions that guide organization, writers can divide and highlight the segments of a document through deliberate headings and subheadings. Long documents require headings; shorter documents are aided by them. A quick glance at headings will allow readers an overview of the larger picture and will show how the picture's pieces fit together. Headings help writers too: If the headings added to the first draft don't make sense or seem repetitive, the writer has the opportunity to make necessary adjustments among the segments. Once in place, the headings help the writer evaluate each section's coherence. Some guidelines:

(1) Headings need to satisfy the needs of your audience. A memorandum labeled "Element One," "Element Two," and "Element Three" offers the reader no insight to content or organization. A heading should identify the material within that block and also summarize an aspect of the analysis. The introductory paragraph below is followed by the three headings anticipated in the set-up:

facts   On July 17, 1989, Mr. William Brown, the plaintiff, was stopped and arrested by municipal police officer John Smith, the defendant, and one other unidentified police officer. The plaintiff alleges that the arrest and the events occurring during the arrest were violations of

law   his civil rights under 42 U.S.C. §1983. In general, that statute states that no person, acting under color of any law, may

3 claims

abridge the freedoms or liberties guaranteed by the laws or by the U.S. Constitution. In his complaint, the plaintiff makes three claims: that his arrest interfered with his exercise of an unnamed First Amendment right, that the defendant's refusal to allow the plaintiff to speak during the arrest was a denial of his First Amendment right to speak, and that he was battered by defendant during the arrest.

headings indicate organizational choices: 3 claims

A. <u>Unnamed rights are not defendable.</u>

. . .

B. <u>A 42 U.S.C. violation of the right to speak is fact-specific.</u>

. . .

C. <u>Excessive force and the charge of battering are defined by statute.</u>

. . .

If you discover that your headings signal an incorrect relationship between parts, you need to correct the draft or risk confusing readers about both the organization of the section and its relationship to the whole.

Try skimming this or another chapter of the book and you will see the need for, and help from, headings: Headings signal a major shift of ideas. By skimming only headings, readers get a sense of the overall picture and its parts; they can stop to read the sections that will resolve their problems.

(2) Headings should be parallel in content, grammar, and placement. One section may contain subheadings while other

sections do not—that is perfectly acceptable. But to insert a major heading before one element of negligence and not before the other two destroys any parallel organization of major ideas. If you highlight all three elements as major headings and then subdivide the element where the facts of your case are important, the subheadings will signal to readers that one element is more complicated or more important to the case.

(3) Headings can consist of single words, phrases, and sentences, but they should be consistent in content and grammatical structure. If the first major heading is a full sentence, then all the other major headings should be full sentences.[1] The subheadings may be only phrases, but then each equivalent subheading should be a phrase.

(4) Headings should be consistent in typography; if major subheadings are flush left and underlined, then sub-subheadings need to be differentiated as a group by a consistent indent or perhaps they should not be underlined. Several courts have specific guidelines for headings, but others do not, so writers need to research before assuming that one format will work for any document.

(5) Headings should be independent of the text that follows them. The following example relies on its lengthy heading for its logic; if the readers skipped the heading, they would find themselves in the middle of a definition of proximate cause that has no context. The writer has left the context back up in the heading and has forgotten to reestablish it within the textual discussion:

---

1. Headings in a brief are more effective if they are written as sentences than merely words or phrases; each heading can summarize an argument rather than introduce the issue.

B. <u>According to MCLA 281.1051, an operator of a vessel has a duty to render reasonable assistance to a person affected by an accident in Michigan lakes and rivers.</u>

However, the relationship is special for another reason, and that is the Marine Safety Act, which states:

> the operator of a vessel involved in a collision, accident or other casualty, and the operator of any other vessel, so far as he can do without serious danger to his own vessel, crew, and passengers, shall render reasonable assistance to a person affected þy the collision, accident, or other casualty. . . .

[Cite.] This very broad statute essentially requires of any and all boaters and boat operators (like Surrey) a Good Samaritan duty to assist boaters in need of such aid, by any means reasonable and necessary.

Practice Evaluating Headings

Read first the introductory paragraphs two students created for the same memorandum. Are their headings, taken out of their original discussions, reasonable follow-ups to their introductions? Then evaluate the readers' subsequent responses to these paragraphs.

1. Devoe's sudden illness will not shield him from liability for the injuries to the passenger. The driver of an automobile is not liable for an accident that injures another person if he is suddenly stricken by an illness, which he has no reason to anticipate, that renders him unable to operate the automobile. [Cohen cite.] Devoe was struck by a sudden illness known as narcolepsy, a disease that suddenly, without warning, places a person in a deep sleep. The main issue centers around the question of whether the sudden attack of the disease was for any reason foreseeable under the circumstances. Another question of this case is whether the narcoleptic attack ren-

dered him unable to drive the automobile. Given the facts as described above, the trial court is likely to determine that the attack and its consequences of unconsciousness that rendered Devoe unable to drive the car were foreseeable.

    A. The "Sudden Illness and Impairment" Requirement
    B. The "Reasonably Foreseeable" Requirement

    2. Mr. Devoe's illness will probably shield him from liability for Mr. Patterson's injuries. The plaintiff unexpectedly fell asleep at the wheel of his car, causing the accident. A person who is suddenly taken ill while driving, and is consequently unable to drive safely, is not liable for negligence unless he could have foreseen his incapacity. [Cohen cite]. In Cohen, a man who suddenly fainted while driving, having no reason to believe that he was likely to do so, was not liable for injuries to his passenger caused by his loss of control of the car and subsequent accident. A narcoleptic like Devoe will be stricken suddenly and without warning. It is worth considering, however, the possibility that Devoe experienced previous, undiagnosed narcoleptic episodes sufficient to establish that he reasonably could have foreseen that a blackout would occur when driving. The court is likely to find that foreseeability is not reasonable.

    A. "Suddenness of Onset" Requirement
    B. "Unable to Foresee Incapacity" Requirement

Readers' Responses

    1. The initial thesis satisfies readers' need for an answer. The Cohen holding is stated clearly. Identification of the two issues ("The main issue . . . foreseeable" and "Another question . . . unable to drive") leads the readers to expect a two-part test, but the headings are not the same two: They are reversed and use different terminology. They fail to fulfill the set-up.

2. Initial thesis centers on negligence. The <u>Cohen</u> holding is clear. But the digression to <u>Cohen</u> facts is not connected to facts of Devoe's problem. The "possibility" of Devoe's earlier experiences is not developed and leaves readers confused. Thus, the two headings within the following discussion do not follow the set-up because the set-up is unclear.

Micro Organization

Today's paragraphs are built on the basic concept that one idea deserves one paragraph.[2] Beyond those modern guidelines, writers have a variety of choices based on their understanding of the audience's education and interest level, on the nature of the material, and finally on their personal choice to create interest and impact.

The importance of topic sentences

Topic sentences work in much the same way as theses (see page 3): They introduce the idea within the paragraph, set boundaries for the paragraph, and help tie paragraphs together through transition. Some paragraphs will not require a specific topic sentence but still need cueing transitions to help readers stay on track.

Quickly skim the following student memorandum and then review the following isolated list of *only* the memorandum's topic sentences, which you can evaluate as the foundation of the memorandum's infrastructure.

---

2. Linguist Richard Larson explains the three categories of paragraph theory:

1. Paragraphs are expanded sentences, governed by syntactical forces.
2. Paragraphs are self-contained units of writing with their own unique principles.
3. Paragraphs are parts of the overall discourse, informed by the strategies a writer chooses for the overall piece.

RICHARD LARSON, TEN BIBLIOGRAPHIC ESSAYS 54 (1987).

MEMORANDUM

TO: Clifford Atterbury

FROM: Charles McFinney

DATE: September 21, 1992

SUBJECT: Intent element of potential battery claim
           against Ann Oakley by Will Cody

QUESTION PRESENTED: Does an actor satisfy the intent element of a battery claim when she causes an unintended harm to an unintended victim?

CONCLUSION: Yes. First, the intent element of a battery action is satisfied against an actor who causes an unintended harm to an unintended victim. Also, if an actor intended to cause a particular harm, her intent in that regard can be transferred to the harm actually resulting from her action. Specific intent is not required with regard to the harm caused or the recipient of the harm. Oakley performed a volitional act with a harmful result, and her intent in performing that volitional act is imputed to the actual harm caused and to the actual recipient of the harm.

FACTS: Oakley surprised two apparent thieves in her oft-robbed pumpkin patch. She ran at them, shouting, and fired two warning shots above and to the right of them. Cody heard the first shot and saw the trespassers fleeing Oakley's property. The second shot struck Cody in the leg. Cody has threatened to sue Oakley for battery, claiming damages of medical expenses and lost wages. Oakley is an excellent shot and probably could have hit the trespassers if that were her intent. Also, Oakley was unaware of Cody's location when she fired the shots.

DISCUSSION: Cody's battery claim against Oakley hinges on the legal issue of the transferability of Oakley's intent in causing the harm inflicted upon Cody. Intent to cause a harm is not limited to the intended recipient of the harm. Specific intent with regard to the particular recipient of the injury is not required in a tort action for assault and battery. Morrow v. Flores, 225 S.W.2d 621, 623-24 (Tex. Civ. App.—Fort Worth 1949, writ ref'd n.r.e.). Also, intent to cause a harm in a tort action is not limited to the actor's intended harm. The actor's intent to cause one harm transfers to satisfy the intent requirement for the harm actually resulting from the act. Bennight v. Western Auto Supply Co., 670 S.W.2d 373, 378 (Tex. App.—Austin 1984, writ ref'd n.r.e.). These rules of law interrelate in the fact pattern presented because this tort action is based on an unintended harm to an unintended recipient of that harm. The court in Morrow, in holding that an actor's intent to shoot a particular person satisfied the intent element of a battery action brought by the actual injured person, extends Oakley's intent to cause harm to the trespassers to the harm caused to Cody. 225 S.W.2d at 624. In Bennight, the court held intent transferred when the manager of an auto supply store intended to cause the harm of apprehension in the victim but instead caused the actual harm of an offensive touch. 670 S.W.2d at 378. This transfer of interest is relevant because Ms. Oakley intended to cause the harm of apprehension of battery but instead caused the actual harm of battery to Mr. Cody. A synthesis of these holdings indicates the intent element of a battery claim against Oakley for causing an unintended harm to an unintended victim should be satisfied.

Requisite intent is an essential element of a battery action. There are two rules of law regarding intent relevant to this case. The first rule of law is concerned with the actor's intent in causing a harm to a person different from the person intended to receive the harm. Intent to cause a harm to one person extends the actor's liability to another, unintended recipient of the harm. <u>Morrow</u>, 225 S.W.2d at 624. An act is intentional if the actor intended to cause harm. That the person injured by the actor's actions was unintended is irrelevant. <u>Id</u>. at 625.

The legal situation in <u>Morrow</u>, like that in Oakley's case, involves a battery action brought by the unintended victim of a shooting. Appellant in the case was involved in pursuing an individual who had damaged his property. When he encountered the individual, they scuffled briefly, and the individual attempted to flee. Appellant, armed with a pistol, shot after the fleeing man, missing him and striking a bystander, Appellee, in the foot. The court held that Appellant, in intending to shoot the third party, demonstrated the intent required for a battery action brought by the unintended recipient of the injury.

The second rule of law deals with the actor's intent in causing a particular harm different from the harm intended. An actor's intent to cause a harm different from the actual harm caused is transferred to the actual harm that did occur. <u>Bennight</u>, 670 S.W.2d at 377. <u>Bennight</u> involved an auto supply store with a bat-infested area in the back. The manager of this store repeatedly required an employee who he knew was apprehensive of the bats to enter this area as a part of her duties of employment. On one such occasion the employee was bitten by a bat. The question before the court was whether the manager's conduct satisfied the intent requirement of a battery claim. The court held the manager intentionally placed the employee in apprehension of being bitten by a bat, and this was an assault. Id. at 379. The court held further the manager's intention to commit this assault against the employee transferred to the specific additional injury that she received, even though the manager may not have intended that subsequent harm. Id. at 380.

Oakley's case is analogous to a synthesis of Morrow and Bennight. Her two defenses to a battery claim are that she did not intend any harm to Cody and she did not intend to cause a battery. She caused an unintended harm to an unintended victim. However, the facts establish Oakley did intend to cause an apprehension of a harm in the two trespassers. There is no evidence that Oakley had any privilege to fire upon these trespassers. Her conduct in intentionally causing this apprehension is analogous to the manager's conduct in Bennight. Although he did not intend a battery against his employee, he did intentionally place the employee in apprehension of a battery, and this was held to be sufficient to sustain a battery claim. Oakley's intent to scare the trespassers constitutes assault, and her intent to commit assault is transferred to the actual harm, battery, caused by her actions. Similarly, Oakley's intent to cause a harm to an intended victim parallels the situation in Morrow. Morrow fired his pistol with the intention of causing a harm to an intended victim, and when his action harmed an unintended victim, he was held liable for his conduct. Oakley also fired her gun with intent to cause a harm to intended victims. Her action harmed an unintended victim, and her intent to cause the harm to an intended victim transfers to the actual recipient of the harm.

A strong counter argument to this conclusion is that such a synthesis of the rules of law in Bennight and Morrow is inappropriate and goes beyond the scope of the courts' holdings. The opinions do not address the issue of the "double transfer" of intent that the synthesis above seems to require. This argument would assert that the cases cited are limited in their application to strictly analogous situations. Since neither court was presented with nor envisioned a scenario where the actor caused an unintended harm to an unintended recipient, an extension of liability under the authority of these cases would be inappropriate.

This counter argument ignores the nature of the transfers of intent and the policy considerations behind the holdings of Bennight and Morrow. The transfers of intent with regard to the intended harm and the intended victim are independent. More compelling, however, are the policy considerations of the cases. Both cases are concerned with discouraging irresponsible behavior that increases the risk of harm to others. Morrow accomplishes this by making an actor liable for his actions beyond the intended recipient. Bennight accomplishes this policy goal by extending an actor's liability to harms different from the harm intended by his actions. It would be inconsistent with these policy goals to have a situation where liability would be reduced in a situation where a person acted so irresponsibly that she caused an unintended harm to an unintended recipient. A combination of the holdings of Bennight and Morrow is consistent with their policy goals and is appropriate. The intent element of a battery claim against Oakley should be satisfied.

Consider this rapid summary of the entire document:

(1) Cody's battery claim against Oakley hinges on the legal issue of the transferability of Oakley's intent in causing the harm inflicted upon Cody. (2) Requisite intent is an essential element of a battery action. (3) The legal situation in Morrow, like that in Oakley's case, involves a battery action brought by the unintended victim of a shooting. (4) The second rule of law deals with the actor's intent in causing a particular

harm different from the harm intended. (5) Oakley's case is analogous to a synthesis of <u>Morrow</u> and <u>Bennight</u>. (6) A strong counter argument to this conclusion is that such a synthesis of the rules of law in <u>Bennight</u> and <u>Morrow</u> is inappropriate and goes beyond the scope of the courts' holdings. (7) This counter argument ignores the nature of the transfers of intent and the policy considerations behind the holdings of <u>Bennight</u> and <u>Morrow</u>.

Most of the sentences are perfect introductions/conclusions to the content of the paragraphs. Read separately, they inform the reader of each step of the analysis. Read together, they form an elliptical but coherent paragraph. As you edit your rough draft, separate each topic sentence from your text and examine each one to make sure it is a strong introduction to the main idea of that paragraph. Then again examine the coherence of the topic sentences as they relate to the overall thesis set-up.

Practice with Topic Sentences

The paragraph below opens an argument on economic waste. Evaluate the paragraph below for its topic sentence and usefulness. If it is ineffective, rewrite it. A suggestion for revision follows.

<u>American Standard</u> mentioned <u>Groves v. John Wunder Co.</u> [cite] in which the cost of completion was $60,000 and the total value of the property was only $12,160. The courts rejected the diminution-in-value rule because it was the owner's right to erect structures that may even reduce the property's value and the result "can be of no aid to any contractor who declines performance." [Cite.] Where, however, the breach is of a covenant that is only incidental to the main purpose of the contract and completion would be disproportionately costly, courts have applied the diminution-in-value rule even where

no destruction of work is entailed. [Cite.] The facts differ in the Babbitts' situation because the breach is not incidental to the purpose of the contract but is the main purpose of the contract.

Suggestion for Revision

A beginning sentence that details a case within a case is not a topic sentence—it provides no overriding perspective. The diminution-in-value rule is clear, but its relation to the "incidental" exception is not clearly drawn in relation to these facts. That the facts differ with the Babbitts is not the conclusion.

Evaluate this student's introductory paragraph (with road map); then compare it to the student's topic sentences that follow. A reader response follows the example.

The court is likely to hold that Devoe is not shielded from liability for the automobile accident. The Court of Appeals of the District of Columbia has held that "one who is (1) suddenly stricken by an illness, (2) which he had no reason to anticipate, while driving an automobile, (3) which renders it impossible for him to control the car, is not chargeable with negligence." [Cite.] In the instant case, the principal issue is whether Devoe had reason to anticipate his sudden lapses into sleep before the accident occurred.

Topic sentences from original:

A. The court is likely to find that Devoe had reason to anticipate his sudden lapse into deep sleep.

B. In a case analogous to ours, the driver of an automobile fainted without anticipation, swerved into an embankment, and injured a passenger.

C. Devoe's automobile became uncontrollable immediately preceding the accident.

Reader Response

Effective conclusion/thesis, and clear three-prong test that appears to be the set-up. The conclusion emphasizes "reason to anticipate" as the main controversy. The first heading, therefore, covers the main controversy and is logical. However, the second heading, referring to facts from another case, offers no connection to either the three prongs or to the "reason to anticipate." The third heading relates to prong three, but the different terminology ("impossible to control the car" versus "automobile became uncontrollable") forces readers to make necessary connections.

Case citations and holdings masquerading as topic sentences

Case names and citation information rarely function as effective topic sentences. When readers begin a paragraph without an effective topic sentence, they cannot assimilate a new case name and citation into what they have just read in the preceding paragraph. Evaluate the following paragraph that begins with a case name:

Jankowski v. Mazzotta, 7 Mich. App. 483, 152 N.W.2d 49 (1967), held that the distinction between cases allowing recovery for mental damages involves those for breach of contract and those for other breaches.

It is difficult to imagine the connection between this paragraph and one that might have led into it. Perhaps if the writer had begun with the holding and followed it with the citation, the holding itself would stand out and provide the transitional bridge for the reader to follow:

The distinction between cases allowing recovery for mental damages involves those for breach of contract and those for other breaches. Jankowski v. Mazzotta, 7 Mich. App. 483, 152 N.W.2d 49 (1967).

Placing the emphasis on the topic sentence information rather than the case name is one way to ensure that paragraphs help cue readers to the overall organizational scheme. An equally useful device is a transition into a new paragraph:

> **Specifically,** the distinction between cases allowing recovery for mental damages involves those for breach of contract and those for other breaches. Jankowski v. Mazzotta, 7 Mich. App. 483, 152 N.W.2d 49 (1967).

> **In contrast to** recovery for actual damages, the distinction between cases allowing recovery for mental damages involves those for breach of contract and those for other breaches. Jankowski v. Mazzotta, 7 Mich. App. 483, 152 N.W.2d 49 (1967).

Special attention is necessary when a paragraph discusses the holdings of two (or more) cases, even if the points of the cases are consistent and supportive. Notice how the weak topic sentences below do not prepare readers for the cases discussed in the paragraphs:

> In oral employment contracts, the courts have held that neither partial nor full performance will be sufficient to take the contract out of the statute of frauds. Mercer v. C.A. Roberts Co., 570 F.2d 1232, 1237 (5th Cir. 1978).
> Similarly, in Paschall v. Anderson, 91 S.W.2d 1050 (Tex. 1936), the court held that full performance was not enough to take the contract out of the statute of frauds. In Chevalier v. Lane's Inc., 213 S.W.2d 530 (Tex. 1948), the court held that part performance is not enough to take an oral contract out of the statute. Later in Collins v. McCombs, 511 S.W.2d 745 (Tex. Civ. App. — San Antonio 1974, writ ref'd n.r.e.), the court reaf-

firmed its stance that full performance will not take an oral employment contract out of the statute of frauds.

The second topic sentence ("Similarly ... ") focuses on *Paschall* but does not anticipate *Chevalier*. Also, if the two cases are "similar" to *Mercer*, the similarity needs to be identified in a topic sentence that points out the larger perspective.

Missing transitions

Transitions may look insignificant, but they are actually a glue that holds documents together; they facilitate logical connections between ideas. Whether connecting large-scale segments, paragraphs, sentences, or words, transitions signal relationships. *Extrinsic transitions* signal relationships in a conscious, traditional manner (*again, once, finally, however*). *Intrinsic transitions*, on the other hand, are stylistic devices such as repetition and dovetailing that glue ideas together without a specific word transition. Without transitions of some kind, your sentences will be choppy, and readers will be forced to make the connections for you.

Readers should be able to trace how writers structure their discussions, descriptions, and arguments simply by isolating the transitions. Writers can evaluate their own transitions by reviewing a finished document: Cut a document into paragraph blocks, scramble the blocks of prose, and quickly reassemble the original document according to its transitions and topic sentences. If the writer has to reread each full paragraph, then the transitions and topic sentences need sharpening.

Similarly, writers can experiment with transitions within a single paragraph by cutting one paragraph into separate sentences, mixing them up, and asking a friend to organize the paragraph again. If the friend cannot reassemble the original, then the writer needs to examine the relationship between sentences and add transitions. The following paragraph effectively uses extrinsic transitions:

Continuous usage and widespread usage by the public are important factors in determining the public's right to an easement in a road; **however,** the measure of these factors is much less clear. **For example**, sixty-five people testifying that they have used a road all of their lives, which was in excess of fifty years, was found to have been widespread and continuous enough. <u>Perkins</u>, 239 S.E.2d at 70. **In contrast,** public usage going back to 1915, characterized by witnesses as "at least several times a week and maybe every day," was found by the court in <u>Stone</u> to be distinguishable from <u>Perkins,</u> in regard to widespread usage. **Although** we do not know if the roads in the <u>Perkins</u> and <u>Stone</u> cases were used only in the summer, one could assume they were, **because** in both cases the roads led to a boat launching area on a river or lake. **Thus,** continuous use in the Trevors' case may possibly be satisfied by the fifteen years of nearly daily summer use **because,** for the entire lifetime of the road in·the Trevors' case, it has been used by the public. **On the other hand,** widespread use is less clear. **In our clients' case,** over twenty people is less than the sixty-five people in <u>Perkins,</u> but potentially more than the number of people in <u>Stone</u>.

Intrinsic transitions

In addition to the extrinsic transitions, there are *intrinsic* transitions: regular words used with the special purpose of gluing ideas together. An obvious example is careful, deliberate *repetition* of ideas to create cohesion ("dovetailing" through words with the same base[3]):

---

3. See, for instance, Anne Enquist's discussion in *The Legal Writing Handbook* 229-230, 541-542, 577-590 (1993).

The concept of "racial discrimination" may be approached from the **perspective** of either its victim or its **perpetrator**. . . . The **perpetrator perspective** presupposes a world composed of atomistic individuals whose actions are outside of and apart from the social fabric and without historical continuity. . . . **It is a world where**, but for the conduct of these misguided ones, the system of equality of opportunity would work to provide a distribution of the good things in life without racial disparities and **where** deprivations that did correlate with race would be "deserved" by those deprived on the grounds of "insufficient merit." **It is a world where** such things as "vested rights," "objective selection systems," and "adventitious decisions" (all of which serve to prevent victims from experiencing any change in conditions) are matters of fate, having nothing to do with the problem of racial discrimination.[4]

Practice with Transitions

After reviewing the following choppy paragraph, add both extrinsic transitions and necessary repetition so that the paragraph has coherence.

In <u>Tyler v. Guerry</u>, 160 S.E.2d 889 (S.C. 1968), the court ruled dedication of the road had not been proved. In <u>Tyler v. Guerry</u>, a limited number of local people had used an old road as access to a river. There they fished and had picnics for more than fifty years. Ten years before the suit, a new road was built for the river. The old road fell into disuse. One of the issues was whether the new road had been dedicated to the public. The Supreme Court did not find it persuasive that the public authorities had supplied labor and equipment to the construction and building of the new road. They ruled that the

---

4. Alan Freeman, *Legitimizing Racial Discrimination Through Antidiscrimination Law: A Critical Review of Supreme Court Doctrine*, 62 MINN. L. REV. 1049, 1051-52 (1978) (emphasis added) (citations omitted).

plaintiff had not met the high standard of proof required to show a dedication. Our case is similar.

Possible Answer

Our case is similar to <u>Tyler v. Guerry</u>, 160 S.E.2d 889 (S.C. 1968), another problem of implied dedication of an **old road**. **The old road** in the city of Tyler led to a river, where a limited number of local people had fished and held picnics for more than **fifty years**. **After all those years** but ten years before the suit, a **new road** was built. Whether **this new road** had been dedicated to the public was one of the issues of the suit that reached the supreme **court**. **The court** ruled that the plaintiff had not met the high standard of proof required to show a dedication. **Specifically,** the **court** did not find it persuasive that the **public authorities** had supplied labor and equipment to the construction and building of the new road. That the **public authorities** supplied labor and equipment is the same argument in our case.

Conclusion

When revising a draft document, legal writers have at their disposal an arsenal of organizational cues to help their readers easily follow the ideas and logic of the final document. Writers choose an appropriate organization by analyzing their readers' needs and expectations, but there is no "right" or "wrong" way to organize; organization embodies both the audience and the message. Your organizational tools should reflect the strategy of your logic: introduction, set-up, thesis, road maps, headings, and transitions. Many writers discover that superimposing this highlighted organization after the first draft helps them rethink their own strategy.

ADDITIONAL EXERCISES
(See Possible Answers in Appendix at page 175.)

1. Road maps or set-ups.   Many readers would not be able to follow the road map paragraph below. Why? What could be done to correct the problem?

> Both Federal Rules of Civil Procedure 26(b)(4)(B) and 26(b)(1) may be applied to determine the discoverability of the identities of persons retained or specifically employed by a party in anticipation who did not expect to be called as witnesses at trial. The two rules will be examined for textual content, the possible intent of the drafters, and policy justifications associated with each.

(*See* Appendix, page 143, for a good memorandum with strong set-up, topic sentences, and thesis.)

2. Order of information.   Using the legal formula taught in your legal writing class, reorganize the following paragraph:

> ❶ In arguing our clients' case, it will be crucial that we prove the Trevors' use of the road is sufficiently analogous to <u>Perkins</u> so that the caveats of <u>Stone</u> should not apply; in this regard, several facts could redound to our benefit. ❷ While our clients used the road for only fifteen years, and only during the summer months, they did use it on a daily basis during those months. ❸ It is possible to infer that the character of the use in <u>Perkins</u> was the same as in our case; ❹ in the previous case, the citizens of Darlington County used the road to reach a sandy, beach-like area where they launched fishing boats and engaged in other recreational activities that could reasonably be construed as seasonal (i.e., summer) in nature. ❺ Moreover, the

concentrated use of the road by the Trevors and their neighbors could be interpreted as being widespread— it almost certainly is more widespread than the use of the road described in Stone.

3. Order and topic sentences.   Rewrite the following draft to gather material into cohesive blocks, adding topic sentences and transition cues as necessary:

In Chamberland v. Parker the plaintiff hired Parker to erect a monument that would reduce the value of his premises. The court held that a duly paid contractor could not decline to build it based on his belief that the monument would not be beneficial to the plaintiff. [Cite.] Later, relying on Parker, the American Standard court said, "[i]t does not lie with a defendant who has been so employed and for building it to say that his own performance would not be beneficial to the plaintiff." [Cite.] In the Babbitts' case Bloat cannot justify nonperformance based on the fact that the higher cabinets and a platform stove may reduce the resale value of the house.

It is likely that the Babbitts paid a higher contract price for the more expensive copper pipe and for the special construction involved in unusually high cabinets and a platform stove. The Babbitts' decision to move is immaterial to the expectation at the outset and throughout the work of the contract on their home. The construction was completed in 1994. Even if the Babbitts could sell the house and move this month, more than a full year has passed during which the Babbitts have not been able to reap the benefits of the higher working surface that they paid for.

Their decision to add to the house may enhance the importance of full performance even if the decision to sell is factored into the significance of the breaches.

Copper pipe may not affect the market value of the house, but it is a significant selling point for potential buyers.

4. Topic sentences. The following student paragraph over-all is very good. It is introduced by a topic sentence, but you can improve the coherence of the draft version.

First of all, the length of time the Trevors have used the road may not be substantial enough. A similar case involved a road whose public nature was established by its use for fifty years. County of Darlington v. Perkins, 239 S.E.2d 69, 70 (S.C. 1977). The court in Darlington found that an easement had been acquired by implied dedication where as many as sixty-five people using a similar road for over fifty years did establish the road's public nature. Id. at 70. However, another case showed that public usage for fifty years is by no means enough in and of itself to in-fer an implied dedication. Stone v. International Paper Co., 359 S.E.2d 83, 85 (S.C. Ct. App. 1987). The court in Stone, upon determining that the volume of traffic was not great, did not find implied dedication even though the road had been used by the public for over fifty years. Id. at 84. This may be helpful to the Trevors' claim by showing that fifty years is simply an arbitrary number. Still, the number of years of public use is rele-vant and must be substantial. Whether or not fifteen years (as in the present claim) is sufficiently substantial is uncertain, but nevertheless is well short of the length referred to in prior cases.

5. Set-up paragraphs and headings. Evaluate the follow-ing introduction and the headings that follow. Are the headings anticipated? Are they effective?

Brown's complaint probably fails to meet the specificity requirement required by the Third Circuit for civil rights actions. Generally, federal courts are lenient in accepting pleadings. The Third Circuit, however, has established a specificity requirement for actions involving civil rights, and several Third Circuit cases have discussed and applied this requirement. Some other considerations, however, weigh against the sufficiency of Brown's request.

1. The General Rule and the Third Circuit's Specificity Requirement
2. Case Law
3. Counter Analysis

6. Transitions. Identify the transitions and evaluate their effectiveness in this passage from F. Ray Marshall's *Labor in the South* (1967):

The TWOC had some immediate success during the spring and summer of 1937. By August 1937, for example, the committee and ACWA had negotiated 29 agreements, covering 23,000 workers, 17,000 of whom were in the textile industry. Resistance to unionism stiffened during the winter, however, and in spite of some successes elsewhere the TWOC reported only about 25,000 workers under contract by the spring of 1938.

In addition to the usual employer opposition, the TWOC faced the beating and kidnapping of organizers, antiunion citizens' committees, the Ku Klux Klan, antiunion religious revivalists and the AFL. The AFL was offering itself to employers and workers as a more respectable alternative. And the TWOC campaign, like almost every effort to unionize the southern textile industry, was interrupted by a recession.

When the TWOC became the Textile Workers' Union of America-CIO in May 1939, it had 858 contracts covering 235,000 workers. A management evaluation in 1939 placed the TWOC's card-carrying membership in the south at about 20 per cent of the region's 350,000 cotton workers, and only 15 per cent paid dues regularly. The union was able to get contracts covering many fewer than this; only 5 per cent of the South's spindles were estimated to have been affected by union contracts, and a third of these were no longer in force by April 1939. An examination of TWUA records reveals an average of about 10,000 members in the south in 1939. The union encountered much more opposition in the south than in the north. Though the southern unions won more elections, the northern locals had many more closed shops, more active contracts, and fewer antiunion complaint cases filed with the NLRB. Herbert J. Lahne said:

> In the South, by the end of 1939, there were indications (such as a falling off in the number of NLRB elections held) that the union had reached the end of the more readily organizable sections of this traditionally difficult territory. . . . If the T.W.U.S. fails in the Southern cotton mills it cannot really succeed elsewhere.

Reorganization. In 1939, the AFL reconstituted the UTW around several federal labor unions and some dissident groups from the CIO. Southerners were prominent in its reorganization, and efforts to reorganize the south played an important part in its plans.

CHAPTER 2

Creating Sentences with Style

> *We can keep knowledge from those who would use [intimidating language] by locking it up, but we can also hide ideas behind language so impenetrable that only those trained to translate it can find them.*
> — *Joseph M. Williams, Style: Ten Lessons in Clarity and Grace 4 (1985)*

This chapter examines the problems that commonly affect the readability of individual sentences within legal prose. When you edit a draft for sentence structure, look for ways to shorten sentences, to move the subject and verb and object closer together, to keep documentation from breaking the textual flow, to make sentences more dynamic through balance, and to craft sentences that move readers easily from one sentence to the next. We will consider six key problems:

1. passives
2. long sentences
3. left-handed sentences
4. awkward citation placement
5. excessive/intrusive quotations
6. faulty parallelism

Passive Voice

> *Rewriting is not virtuous. It isn't something that ought to be done. It is simply something that most writers find they have to do to discover what they have to say and how to say it.*
> —*Donald Murray, Learning by Teaching: Selected Articles on Writing and Teaching 69 (1982)*

Most of us have been taught that we should avoid the passive voice, but few remember what it is or why it's better to avoid it. A quick review: A verb is "active" when the subject of the sentence is performing the action—"The court held that the defendant was negligent." If the subject is acted upon by something else (as this very clause demonstrates), the verb is "passive"—"It was held that the defendant was negligent."[1]

Overuse or inadvertent use of the passive voice causes several problems:

---

1.   Many students appear to understand passives but confuse the passive voice with a past tense:

The attorney had defended this client. *(not passive, merely past perfect tense)*

Other writers, interested in avoiding the passive, confuse the active "to be," used as a linking verb, with the passive voice:

Clark and Clark is preparing today's brief. *("is preparing" is an active, linking verb — not a passive)*

Even the passive voice can have several tenses:

The campaign is being run by the Democrats at Large. *(passive, present progressive)*
The unsuspecting client was hit by an enormous bill. *(passive, past tense)*

As you edit for passives, then, remember that although the passive voice always includes a form of the "to be" verb, not all "to be" verbs are passive. Likewise, not all passives are bad or incorrect.

- The passive adds unnecessary words.
- The passive steals the punch from active verbs.
- The passive can create ambiguity.
- The passive can misplace sentence emphasis.

Adding unnecessary words

The passive voice adds unnecessary length to sentences when writers use the "to be" verb form and place the actor in a prepositional phrase.

> The award was given to Terri Miller by the Arizona Bar Association. (*12 words*)
>
> REVISION
>
> The Arizona Bar Association gave Terri Miller the award. (*9 words*)

Stealing the punch

Because the actor is not the subject, a passive verb pulls its punch rather than striking with a strong, forceful verb:

> The plaintiff was severely hurt by the defendant's car.
>
> REVISION
>
> The defendant's car crippled (paralyzed, injured) the plaintiff.

Adding ambiguity

Perhaps the most destructive result of the passive voice occurs in a *truncated passive*, where the agent of the action is missing altogether and the sentence is thus ambiguous:

> The pedestrian **was hit** several times. (*The subject did not perform the action, and the verb has no direct object.*)

REVISION

The defendant's car **hit** the pedestrian several times.
(The subject, "car," did the hitting.)

The truncated passive structure forces readers to draw their own conclusions, which may be wrong.

Misplacing emphasis

A truncated passive may inadvertently emphasize a minor character and place him (or it) at the center of the stage. In the following example, the passive voice confuses the connection between the airplane's physical invasion and the tort of trespass:

In <u>Schronk</u> the defendant's plane was flown low over the plaintiff's land during the crop dusting operation.

REVISION

In <u>Schronk</u> the defendant flew his plane low over the plaintiff's land during the crop dusting operation.

In the original, the plane is guilty, but the pilot is nowhere on the scene. If the writer had used the active voice, the reader could have more easily made the connection of liability. The style of the sentence (passive) leaves a substantive ambiguity. Written in the active voice, the sentence would direct the court to focus on the question of intent to trespass rather than on what agent or thing trespassed.

Using passive voice artfully

Remember that the passive voice can be used deliberately for a specific purpose:

- When you *do not know* the agent/actor ("The girl was propelled out of the train").

- When you need to *protect* your "subject" from a direct accusation ("Marta was dismissed from law school").

- When you want to *emphasize the result* of an action ("George was murdered by a drunken driver").

Artfully crafted passives occur infrequently, but it would be shortsighted to ignore the obvious logic of your sentence structure and omit an effective use of passive voice merely to conform to an arbitrary style suggestion.[2]

Practice Eliminating Passive Voice

Switch the following passive constructions into the active voice.

1. It can be shown through the evidence that . . .

2. The right to trial by jury in administrative license revocation proceedings was recently considered by this court in <u>Adams v. Texas State Board of Chiropractic Examiners</u>, 744 S.W.2d 648 (Tex. App.–Austin 1988, no writ).

---

2.   An example of the passive voice used deliberately comes from Douglas Laycock, Professor of Law at the University of Texas, who wrote the following sentence for a law review:

> This argument was first raised by Kimball, refuted in some detail by Brilmayer, and largely conceded in Kimball's reply.

His law review editor changed all of the passives into active voice but unnecessarily created ambiguity:

> Kimball first raised this argument; Brilmayer refuted it in some detail; and Kimball largely conceded it in his reply.

Laycock's goal was to trace the history of an argument, and his original sentence structure paralleled that goal—the evolution of the ideas, not the originators of them. The agents, deliberately buried in the prepositions after the verbs, were incidental to the thrust of the sentence. The editor's rewrite emphasizes the people rather than the argument and thus creates ambiguity. In the edited constructions "refuted it" and "conceded it," does "it" refer to the original argument or Brilmayer's refutation?

3. (*From a probation officer's testimony:*) During a hearing outside the presence of a jury on Keeling's motion to suppress the identification testimony, it was established that Hartman was currently on deferred adjudication probation for theft over $200.00.

Possible Answers

1. The evidence can show that . . .

2. This court recently considered the right to trial by jury in administrative license revocation proceedings in Adams v. Texas State Board of Chiropractic Examiners, 744 S.W.2d 648 (Tex. App.—Austin 1988, no writ).

3. During a hearing outside the presence of a jury on Keeling's motion to suppress the identification testimony, the probation officer testified that Hartman was currently on deferred adjudication probation for theft over $200.00.

Evaluate the following sentences to decide if recasting the verb into the active voice would strengthen the sentences.

1. The loan was approved by the Lincoln Bank Board of Directors and was on file as an official record of the depository institution.

Leave passive _____ Make active _____

2. Defendants contend that evidence of any purchases made by Plaintiff as a result of the May 19, 1992, press release are barred by the relevant statute of limitations inasmuch as Plaintiff knew, or should have known, of the alleged misrepresentations or omissions contained in the press release by July 1992 when an explanation of the subject press release was published by Company, Inc.

Leave passive _____ Make active _____

3. This theme was broadened by the United States Supreme Court in Tully v. Griffin, Inc., where it was held by the Court that a federal court is "under an equitable duty" to

not interfere with a state's collection of its revenue except when "an asserted federal right might otherwise be lost."

Leave passive _____ Make active _____

Possible Answers

1. Leave passive if the emphasis is on the loan. If the emphasis is on Lincoln's Board of Directors, then switch to active and rewrite:

> The Lincoln Bank Board of Directors approved the loan, which went on file as an official record of the depository institution.

2. Make dependent clauses active.

> Defendants contend that the relevant **statute of limitations bars** evidence of any purchases Plaintiff made as a result of the May 19, 1992, press release because Plaintiff knew, or should have known, of the alleged misrepresentations or omissions contained in the press release by July 1992 when **Company, Inc., published** an explanation of the subject press release.

3. Keep as written if the emphasis is on the theme. Or make active.

> The United States Supreme **Court broadened** this theme in <u>Tully v. Griffin, Inc.</u> **The Court held** that a federal court is "under an equitable duty" to not interfere with a state's collection of its revenue except when "an asserted federal right might otherwise be lost."

The following examples contain typically truncated and thus ambiguous passives. Could readers intuit the necessary actor and thus understand the ambiguity without an actor's being mentioned?

1. It might be said that

Yes_____ No_____

2. The funds were distributed by Terri Miller at the closing by delivering a check to Savings and Loan. In addition, a check was paid to McDonald and another check was paid to The Insurance Company.

Yes_____ No_____

3. Pursuant to your request, enclosed are copies of the State Pattern Jury Charges that will be adapted for submission to the jury at the trial of the captioned matter.

Yes_____ No_____

Possible Answers

1. No. *(ambiguous — who might say?)*

2. Yes/No. Terri Miller distributed. Who paid the checks to McDonald and Insurance Company? *(ambiguous)*

3. No. Who will adapt the Charges: perhaps the readers, perhaps the court at the time of trial. *(ambiguous)*

Long Sentences

> There are only two cures for the long sentence:
> (1) Say less;
> (2) Put a period in the middle.
> Neither expedient has taken hold in the law.
> — David Mellinkoff, The Language of the Law 366 (1963)

Legal writers' sentences are frequently long because legal training emphasizes qualifying each factor with additional evidence. This practice can force essential information into a chain of clauses and thereby create long, convoluted sentences. Not all long sentences are difficult, of course; no set number of words or typed lines breaks readability rules. If the sentences are carefully punctuated and cued, then all those necessary qualifications may reasonably appear within a sentence or two and not affect the document's readability. Without proper cueing, though, a chain of clauses will confuse readers:

The Court of Appeals, Cummings,

"that instruction that if"?

Circuit Judge, held **that** instruction **that**

another "that if plaintiff"!

if jury found **that if** plaintiff stored

property in good condition in

defendant's warehouse **and** the property

was returned in damaged condition,

"recovery"—there's more?

plaintiffs were entitled to recovery

"unless"—here we go again.

unless jury found that defendant

"to prevent . . . to explain"—I'm lost.

exercised ordinary care and diligence **to**

prevent damage to the property **was**

"was sufficient"— what's the subject here?

sufficient to explain Illinois law on

burden of proof in bailment cases **and,** in absence of instruction that plaintiffs had ultimate burden of proof with respect to defendant's fault, defendant was entitled to a reversal. <u>Celanese Corp. of America v. Vandalia Warehouse Corp.</u>, 424 F.2d 1176 (7th Cir. 1970) (emphasis added).

Here are a few solutions for excessively long sentences:

1. Where possible, move chains of subordinate clauses into separate independent clauses or sentences.
2. Avoid excessive coordination and subordination.
3. Place the subject close to the verb, and place both of them toward the beginning of the sentence; after the main subject and verb, follow with the object and qualifying material.
4. If the sentence length is absolutely necessary, then add signposts:
   a. Punctuate to allow for closure.
   b. Add signal words.
   c. Tabulate parallel lists and ideas.

Don't be afraid of short sentences

James Kilpatrick, a political commentator, refers to the "portmanteau syndrome," the habit of packing everything the writer knows into a single traveling bag with ties, socks, and shirttails sticking out because the bag (i.e., sentence) is asked to contain more than it was designed to hold. His cure?

> When I went into newspapering in 1941, I too was afflicted with the portmanteau syndrome. Charles H. Hamilton, who was then city editor of *The Richmond* (Va.) *News Leader*, dispelled the affliction in a note he left on my desk:

> Kilpo:
>> I have something for you:
>> ....
>> Those interesting objects are called periods. They are formed by the second key from the right on the bottom row of your typewriter. Please put them to good use.
>> CHH[3]

Don't worry about rendering sentences too short and choppy; a lot of room exists between the extremes of tiny, choppy sentences and the clause-chain monsters that garble traditional court decisions and contracts.

Break embedded clauses into independent sentences

Ideas tucked into a series of clauses frequently lose their power because these mini-sentences interrupt the main clause. It is as if legal writers need to get in every qualifying thought about the main idea before they stop and signal "it is over" with a period. The result is both an overloaded sentence and an exhausted reader. Look at the sentence below with nine nouns and six verbs. How does the reader know what is important?

> In an attempt to mitigate the harshness of this doctrine, the courts developed the idea of constructive eviction **whereby** a tenant could assert **that** the condi-

---

3. JAMES KILPATRICK, THE WRITER'S ART 88 (1984).

tion of the premises was such **that** they were unlivable **and** therefore he had been "constructively evicted" by his landlord.

REVISION

In an attempt to mitigate the harshness of this doctrine, the courts developed the idea of "constructive eviction." [*New sentence:*] A tenant could assert **that** the condition of the premises was unlivable and therefore **that** he had been "constructively evicted" by his landlord.

OR

A tenant could assert **that** the condition of the premises was unlivable; **thus**, he follows the court-created idea **that** he was "constructively evicted" by his landlord.

Investigating your own clauses within long sentences, you may discover you have simply packed too many important qualifiers into one sentence. Revise until the ideas of importance stand on their own and aren't hidden away inside disruptive clauses.

Avoid excessive coordination and subordination

Legal writers also create unnecessarily long sentences if they use *excessive coordination*. Ideas are strung together with "and" and "or" until the writer has covered every qualifying idea and fact, but not before the reader has run out of breath. Coordination forces readers through too much parallel information—all in a sing-song rhythm. *Excessive subordination*, on the other hand, creates readability problems because the dependent clauses interfere with the main textual message and occasionally modify each other instead of the main idea. Subordinate clauses can also separate the subject and verb, burying important ideas under layers of intervening clauses:

If the neighbor has caused pecuniary loss **or** substantial inconvenience to the Company **or** a third person, this cause is available **if** the neighbor has, without the effective consent of the Company, intentionally **or** knowingly tampered with its tangible property.

A rewrite of this sentence would have to untangle the coordinate and subordinate clauses, and help readers understand which idea each "if" clause modifies. Perhaps separating the subordinates with numbers will help:

This cause is available (1) **if** the neighbor has intentionally or knowingly tampered with the Company's tangible property without the effective consent of the Company and (2) **if** the neighbor has caused pecuniary loss or substantial inconvenience to the Company or a third person.

Keep the subject close to its verb

Readers need closure through either punctuation or syntax. English sentence order is fairly simple (subject/verb/object, plus a few variations with clauses) because, unlike heavily conjugated foreign languages, the sense of an English sentence depends on the logical relationship of these three parts of a sentence. If legal writers separate the English subject from its verb by clauses and citations, their readers have more trouble decoding the relationship between the words and may have to reread the sentence.

Taxpayer's failure to identify what rentals of unmanned logging units, if any, involved nontaxable services as opposed to taxable rentals of unmanned logging units to logging companies or to oil companies with their own engineers or geologists **prevents** it from overcoming the presumption of taxability and correctness of the audit.

The above example can be improved by either (1) moving the subject and verb together or (2) eliminating unnecessary words and redrafting passive constructions into the active:

> **Taxpayer cannot overcome the presumption** of taxability and correctness for the following reason: . . .

Another unfortunate result of an unnatural separation between subject and verb is verb agreement problems:

> The undersigned **officers**, each a responsible Officer of Singleton Drilling Company, a Delaware corporation, Singleton Oil and Gas Company, a Delaware corporation, and Singleton Drilling International, Inc., a Delaware corporation (each a "Borrower" and collectively "Borrowers"), hereby **certifies** that as such, he is authorized to execute this Certificate on behalf of such respective Borrower.

Add signposts to long sentences

Careful signposting is another stylistic technique to defeat the confusion of long sentences. Words can be signposts when they signal relationships: transitions, repetitions of words or phrases, introductions, and conclusions. Most of us would rather not read the following sentence, taken from a law review, because it is long and dense; but at least its message is accessible because its signposts guide readers through the relationships and clauses:

> **If** we endeavor to find from within legal education a conception of successful legal education, **and hence** the prevailing conception of the good lawyer, a dominant, quite familiar answer is there: Legal education, **when** it is done successfully and well, will produce graduates **who** will be good lawyers, technically proficient **in, at, and with** the law—**persons who** under-

stand how to engage in legal analysis and the construction and assessment of legal argument, **who** understand and can employ adeptly and imaginatively legal doctrines and concepts, **and who** can and will bring skills and knowledge of this sort regularly and fully to bear upon any matter of concern to any client willing and able to employ them **in order to further** the client's interest, **provided only** that they, as lawyers, do not do what the law prohibits lawyers from doing for clients.[4]

In addition to words used as signposts, punctuation can also function as signposts, making the message more accessible:

The Comptroller cannot be bound to follow the erroneous advice of his agent for two reasons: The taxpayer has the burden of proving the affirmative advice was affirmatively given, and the taxpayer must show that the agent was aware of all the circumstances and yet advised him on an erroneous course of taxable action.

The colon and the commas clearly establish the relationship between ideas within this long sentence.

In addition to word and punctuation signposts, writers of dense legal material can use numbered lists (tabulation) to cue the reader to an organizational hierarchy (and add white space to the page). Try following this example, for instance, from an attorney to a company representative for his client, "DIC," and then contrast it to the revised version.

We have heretofore discussed in principle the undersigned's ("DIC") proposal to retain your services in

---

4. Richard Wasserstrom, *Legal Education and the Good Lawyer*, 34 J. LEGAL EDUC. 155, 156 (1984) (emphasis added).

connection with the development of conceptual schemes and preliminary designs for the project, including your review and analysis of the presentation material (plans, sections, audio/visual presentations, renderings, and models) for all meetings with neighborhood groups and appropriate representatives of the city of Dallas, in connection with the proposed application by DIC for rezoning (the "Rezoning") of the Site to a higher residential zoning classification deemed economically feasible to DIC (the "Schematic Design Work").

REVISION

We have already discussed in principle the undersigned's ("DIC") proposal to retain your services to develop conceptual schemes and preliminary designs for the project. These services include

(1) your review and analysis of the Site and the local zoning ordinances, and

(2) the preparation of presentation material (plans, sections, audio/visual presentations, renderings, and models) for all meetings with neighborhood groups and appropriate representatives of the city of Dallas.

You will assist DIC in applying for rezoning (the "Rezoning") of the Site to a higher residential zoning classification deemed economically feasible to DIC ("the Schematic Design Work").

Thus punctuation, tabulation, and signpost words can work with the traditional closure signals to aid long sentences.

When is a sentence too long?

No one has devised a fool-proof formula for the correct sentence length (although the Flesch Index is helpful[5]). Many writers develop their own rule; for instance, for some writers eight lines become immediately suspect, and for others anything over 25 words needs revision.

When you examine sentences for length, be careful not to assume that short sentences are always clear or that long ones are always muddled. Instead, double-check each sentence in your draft for qualities other than length that can create confusion.

Remember:

- Clarity is more important than sentence length.
- If you need to write a long sentence, be considerate of your readers and add signposts: signal words, tabulation, and punctuation.

---

5.   RUDOLF FLESCH, HOW TO WRITE PLAIN ENGLISH: A BOOK FOR LAWYERS AND CONSUMERS 20-25 (1979).   Flesch's formula is designed to indicate the difficulty of your prose as reflected through sentence length and word length. Here is how to use the formula: Test only your own (not quoted) writing.

1.   Count the words in a paragraph (etc.).
2.   Count the symbols, abbreviations, figures, and their combinations as one-syllable words.
3.   Count the sentences, including complete clauses set off by semicolons, dashes, colons, and question and exclamation marks.
4.   Figure the average number of syllables per word.   Divide the number of syllables by the number of words.
5.   Figure the average number of words per sentence.
6.   Find the readability score. Multiply the average sentence length by 1.015. Multiply the average word length by 84.6. Add the two numbers. Subtract this sum from 206.835. This balance is your readability score.

The scale is 0 to 100, with 0 being practically unreadable and 100 being very easy. 0-30 is very difficult; 50-60, fairly difficult; 70-80, fairly easy; 80-90, easy; and 90-100, very easy. Flesch's minimum for plain English writing is 60, or about 20 words per sentence and 1 and 1/2 syllables per word.   After determining your average, compare the results to your audience's abilities: a client, a judge, a senior partner may require different reading levels. Flesch breaks down the scale into education levels also.

Practice Controlling Long Sentences

Evaluate the length of the following sentences and either (1) justify leaving them at their current length or (2) choose one of the following methods to create a more understandable sentence: break into separate sentences, punctuate for clarity, add signposts, position subject and verb closer together, tabulate.

1. <u>Klopps v. Adonis</u>, unlike the kind of in rem action typified by <u>Harris v. Balk</u>, 198 U.S. 215 (1905), in which the property attached was an intangible debt owed by one person to another, involves a tangible form of property.

2. WHEREFORE, the Attorney General, on behalf of the State, prays this Court reverse that portion of the judgment of the County Court Number 2 of Green County entered June 24, 1991, which denied reimbursement to the State for public assistance provided for the support of the subject child, and, because there were no disputed fact issues and the trial court found that the State would be entitled to the full amount of reimbursement but for the application of State Family Code Section 13.42(a) (Tr. 29 [nos. 5&6]), render judgment against Appellee for the State in the amount of $4,655.00 <u>plus</u> interest pursuant to Family Code Section 14.062(a) as reimbursement for public assistance provided, and remand the cause to the trial court to determine an appropriate amount of periodic or lump sum payments on that judgment.

3. Although application of the doctrine of estoppel, upon which apparent authority is based, requires that the person estopped have had knowledge of all material facts at the time of the conduct giving rise to the estoppel, such knowledge may be imputed where the party against whom estoppel is asserted has knowledge of facts sufficient to put him on inquiry which if reasonably pursued would lead to the discovery of the controlling fact.

Possible Answers

1. Re-position subject and verb and break into two sentences.

> <u>Klopps v. Adonis</u> involves a tangible form of property. <u>Klopps</u> differs from the in rem action typified by <u>Harris v. Balk</u>, 198 U.S. 215 (1905), in which the property attached was an intangible debt owed by one person to another.

2. Tabulate and balance the coordination (even in a prayer).

> WHEREFORE, the Attorney General, on behalf of the State, prays this Court
>
> (1)   reverse that portion of the judgment of the County Court Number 2 of Green County entered June 24, 1991, which denied reimbursement to the State for public assistance provided for the support of the subject child,
>
> (2)   render judgment against Appellee for the State in the amount of $4,655.00 <u>plus</u> interest pursuant to State Family Code Section 14.062(a) as reimbursement for public assistance provided because there were no disputed fact issues and the trial court found that the State would be entitled to the full amount of reimbursement but for the application of State Family Code Section 13.42(a) (Tr. 29 [nos. 5&6]), and
>
> (3)   remand the cause to the trial court to determine an appropriate amount of periodic or lump sum payments on that judgment.

3. Break excessive dependent clauses and punctuate nonrestrictive clauses.

> Application of the doctrine of estoppel, upon which apparent authority is based, requires that the person

estopped have had knowledge of all material facts at
the time of the conduct giving rise to the estoppel.
This knowledge may be imputed where the party
against whom estoppel is asserted has knowledge of
facts sufficient to put him on inquiry that, if reasonably pursued, would lead to the discovery of the
controlling fact.

**Find the verbs in the following sentences. How can they be
moved so that readers can more easily recognize the sub-
ject/verb relationship?**

1. The Supreme Court of Florida, following the United
States Supreme Court's lead in providing guidelines only in
the form of what are <u>not</u> permissible excuses for peremptory
challenges by the state, has added the three-part test.

2. In the event of a default on a payment, the entire
amount of an employer's withdrawal liability plus accrued interest on the total outstanding liability from the due date of the
first payment which was not timely made becomes due immediately. 29 U.S.C. § 1399(c)(5).

Possible Answers

1. The Supreme **Court** of Florida **has added** the three-
part test, following the United States Supreme Court's lead in
providing guidelines only in the form of what are <u>not</u>
permissible excuses for peremptory challenges by the state.

2. In the event of a default on a payment, the entire
amount becomes due immediately. This **total includes** an
employer's withdrawal liability plus accrued interest on the
total outstanding liability from the due date of the first payment **that was not timely made**. 29 U.S.C. § 1399(c)(5).

**The following sentences are victims of excessive coordination.
Rewrite them by either (1) breaking each sentence into more
than one sentence, (2) tabulating the elements, or (3) restructur-**

ing the sentence so that the coordination does not intrude into the sentence's meaning.

1. With proper rules, the nonstatutory breed registries (e.g., Appaloosa, Arabians, etc.) could lose their registry status or have their animals barred from pari-mutuel competitions if their members and registered animals are regularly involved in unregistered meets or illegal activities related to racing.

2. The main issues before this Court are whether the taxes, encompassed by the Comptroller's Proof of Claim, to which the Trustee has objected, are (1) either taxes which are "required to be collected or withheld and for which the Debtor is liable in whatever capacity," within the meaning of 11 U.S.C. § 507(a)(7)(C), or "excise" taxes under 11 U.S.C. § 507(a)(7)(E) and (2) whether the actual collection of the taxes is required for such priority treatment.

3. Section 151.056 distinguishes between a lump sum contract and a separated contract and a contractor's tax obligations under the Sales, Excise and Use Tax Chapter of the Tax Code.

Possible Answers

1. With proper rules, the nonstatutory breed registries (e.g., Appaloosa, Arabians, etc.) could lose their registry status **or** have their animals barred from pari-mutuel competitions. **These penalties** would be imposed if the registries' members and registered animals are regularly involved in unregistered meets or illegal activities related to racing.

2. The main issues before this Court **are**

   (1) **whether** the taxes, encompassed by the Comptroller's Proof of Claim, to which the Trustee has objected, either are taxes **that are** "required to be collected or withheld and for which the Debtor is liable in whatever capacity," within the meaning of

11 U.S.C. § 507(a)(7)(C), **or are** "excise" taxes under 11 U.S.C. § 507(a)(7)(E), and

(2) **whether** the actual collection of the taxes is required for such priority treatment.

3. Section 151.056 distinguishes between a lump sum contract and a separated contract that has a contractor's tax obligations under the Sales, Excise and Use Tax Chapter of the Tax Code.

OR

Section 151.056 distinguishes among a lump sum contract, a separated contract, and a contractor's tax obligations under the Sales, Excise and Use Tax Chapter of the Tax Code.

Left-Handed Sentences

The chief object of education is not to learn things but to unlearn them.
—G.K. Chesterton

Sentences that place qualifying or descriptive information before the main subject and its verb are called "left-handed" sentences. They are the hardest long sentences to read because readers have difficulty processing introductory dependent material before they have a context for it; they are forced to read through it, hold it in abeyance, and then place those introductory words in context:

Based on a review of the material regarding the Worker's Compensation Joint Insurance Fund that re- sulted in the Agency's granting of an exemption for a similar fund in 1984 and the material submitted by the expert at our meeting, in my opinion the above-captioned **funds meet** the requirements for exemption as a government entity organization.

To reach the point of this sentence, readers have to absorb 39 words before the beginning of the main clause—and the main subject is *still* hidden behind the superfluous "in my opinion." Because the main idea of this sentence is hidden, readers must reread the whole sentence to properly understand that the goal of the sentence is to communicate that the *funds* in question *meet* an exemption requirement.

The editing of left-handed sentences allows writers to refocus on their priorities. Quick cures for a left-handed sentence are to (1) break the sentence into two sentences and (2) flip-flop the sentence so that the main subject and verb precede the explanatory phrase:

REVISIONS: SEPARATE SENTENCE IDEAS

The above-captioned **funds meet** the requirements for exemption as a government entity organization. **This opinion** is based on a review of the material regarding the Worker's Compensation Joint Insurance Fund that resulted in the Agency's granting of an exemption for a similar fund in 1984 and the material submitted by the expert at our meeting.

OR DISTINGUISH BETWEEN MAIN
AND DEPENDENT CLAUSES

The above-captioned **funds meet** the requirements for exemption as a government entity organization, **which is an opinion** based on a review of the material regarding the Worker's Compensation Joint Insurance Fund that resulted in the Agency's granting of an exemption for a similar fund in 1984 and the material submitted by the expert at our meeting.

Practice Reorganizing Left-Handed Sentences

Experiment with flip-flopping the sentences. Then break them into separate sentences. Which reads more smoothly for each example?

1. If the juror and the defendant are of the same socio-economic class, or if the juror is in a higher class than the defendant, depending on the voir dire and the nature of the case, perhaps the juror will be more sympathetic and more disposed to give the defendant a break.

2. After the Commission's general counsel noted that the Town would have the opportunity to contest the necessity for the proposed treatment facilities at the upcoming hearing on the District's application for an amendment to its wastewater discharge permit, the Commission declined to delay a decision on the District's application.

Possible Answers

1. (*No frame of reference offered readers.*) Perhaps the juror will be more sympathetic and more disposed to give the defendant a break if the juror and the defendant are of the same socio-economic class, or if the juror is in a higher class than the defendant, depending on the voir dire and the nature of the case.

Perhaps the juror will be more sympathetic and more disposed to give the defendant a break if the juror and the defendant are of the same socio-economic class. The juror may also give the defendant a break if the juror is in a higher class than the defendant, depending on the voir dire and the nature of the case.

2. (*Readers discover too late that the decision is delayed.*) The Commission declined to delay a decision on the District's application after the Commission's general counsel noted that the Town would have the opportunity to contest the necessity for the proposed treatment facilities at the upcoming hearing on the District's application for an amendment to its wastewater discharge permit.

The Commission declined to delay a decision on the District's application. The Commission's general counsel had noted that the Town would have the opportunity to contest the necessity for the proposed treatment facilities at the upcoming hearing on the District's application for an amendment to its wastewater discharge permit.

Awkward Citation Placement

> *Courts have bluntly said that about 25 percent of appellate cases revolve around problems of interpretation of language, incomplete negotiation by the parties, and poor draftsmanship either by the parties or their counsel.*
> —*Harold Shepard, Book Review, 1 J. Legal Educ. 151, 154 (1948).*

Citations are a distinctive characteristic of legal writing. They are important, and their form is generally compact (compared to the old Modern Language Association's footnote form), but citations can intrude on textual flow and impede reading comprehension. A citation's greatest virtue is merely its documentation of a legal point. Do not let it get in the way of the expository or persuasive element of the paper.

A citation used as the sentence's subject gives prominence to the case name rather than to the principle of law.

Kewin v. Massachusetts Mut. Life Ins. Co., 295 N.W.2d 50 (Mich. 1980), held that disability insurance contracts are primarily commercial, due to their monetary nature, rather than personal.

Similarly, a new paragraph that leads with a case name leads the reader nowhere; the case name and case summary are not a useful topic sentence:

Clark v. J.M. Benson Co., 789 F.2d 282 (4th Cir. 1986), involved a bookkeeper who took over the responsibilities of company controller. The Fourth Circuit held that because her initial position of bookkeeper was non-administrative she was not exempt from the Fair Labor Standards Act unless the duties as controller comprised over 50 percent of her time. Clark, 789 F.2d at 287.

Just as disturbing as a paragraph beginning with a case name is a paragraph crammed with several citations in a row. Too many citations in prominent places impel readers to disregard the whole string, and thus they miss the point of the sentence. Then the verb pops up without any apparent subject:

Complete diversity of citizenship must exist between parties. Strawbridge v. Curtiss, 7 U.S. 267 (1806). Gordon v. Steele, 376 F. Supp. 575 (W.D. Pa. 1974), held that it is citizenship at the time of filing suit that is controlling.

As an experienced legal reader, you will frequently skim right over citations like the ones in the example above, much like runners jump the hurdles on their way to the finish line, but with back-to-back citations you will miss the subject of the second sentence and have to reread. As a new legal writer, your job is to help readers focus on the important points of your text.

Avoiding graceless citation placement

Moving citations into prepositional phrases or to the end of sentences can allow writers to emphasize the particular court, if it is important:

The United States Supreme Court, in <u>Strawbridge v. Curtiss</u>, 7 U.S. 267 (1806), established the principle that complete diversity of citizenship must exist between parties.

The United States Supreme Court established the principle that complete diversity of citizenship must exist between parties. <u>Strawbridge v. Curtiss</u>, 7 U.S. 267 (1806).

Legal writers have the following options to replace disastrous citation placement in a sentence such as the following:

<u>Sadler v. Musicland-Pickwick Int'l, Inc.</u>, 31 Fed. R. Serv. 2d (Callaghan) 760 (E.D. Tex. 1980), narrowed the test to "relative difficulty" and repetition of steps by both parties.

- **Move the citation into a preposition:**

  The court, in <u>Sadler v. Musicland-Pickwick Int'l, Inc.</u>, 31 Fed. R. Serv. 2d (Callaghan) 760 (E.D. Tex. 1980), narrowed the test to "relative difficulty" and repetition of steps by both parties.

- **Move the citation into an absolute:**

  The test was narrowed to "relative difficulty" and repetition of steps by both parties by a federal court. <u>Sadler v. Musicland-Pickwick Int'l, Inc.</u>, 31 Fed. R. Serv. 2d (Callaghan) 760 (E.D. Tex. 1980).

- **Move the citation out of the sentence:**

  A federal court narrowed the test to "relative difficulty" and repetition of steps by both parties. <u>Sadler v.</u>

Musicland-Pickwick Int'l, Inc., 31 Fed. R. Serv. 2d (Callaghan) 760 (E.D. Tex. 1980).

Instructors repeatedly warn against introducing a case, a holding, or facts without identifying the source right away. Good advice. No reader could accept as accurate a legal argument without documentation. However, place the documentation out of the way of the text itself. Citation placement is not citation deletion. Writers should not omit the citation altogether just to avoid the result of graceless citation placement. Location of citations is actually a matter of politeness.

A final note about the abbreviations that make up citations: They are forms of documentation but not part of the text. Looking through any edition of *The Bluebook*, you will not find examples of a citation form used as a noun in a textual sentence. All of those sentences you have read that begin "In Fed. R. Civ. Proc. . . ." are technically incorrect. The abbreviation is correct within a citation entry, but it is not correct as a substitute for a noun within a sentence. Within a textual sentence, spell out the full words.[6]

Practice Placing Citations

Move or change the following citations using the above suggestions.

1. Although the federal rules require only that the complaint make a "short and plain statement of the claim showing that the pleader is entitled to relief," Fed. R. Civ. Proc. 8(a)(2), the Supreme Court has interpreted that phrase to mean the complaint must provide the defendant with "fair notice of what the plaintiff's claim is and the grounds upon which it rests," Conley v. Gibson, 355 U.S. 41, 47 (1957). The Third Circuit court has taken a somewhat narrower view of what constitutes

---

6.   *See* THE BLUEBOOK: A UNIFORM SYSTEM OF CITATION Rule 10.2.1(c) (15th ed. 1991).

a valid complaint. <u>Rotolo v. Burough of Charleroi</u>, 532 F.2d 920 (3rd Cir. 1976).

2. Quasi-in-rem jurisdiction was first based on the conceptual basis of state sovereignty. <u>Pennoyer v. Neff</u>, 95 U.S. 714 (1878), held that a state has sovereign power over property and persons within its borders, and over nothing outside of them. Thus a state could legitimately require a nonresident to come into the state to defend a cause of action, or forfeit his forum property. <u>Shaffer v. Heitner</u>, 433 U.S. 186 (1977), held that all assertions of state court power must meet standards of due process as articulated in another Supreme Court case, <u>International Shoe v. Washington</u>, 326 U.S. 310 (1945).

3. 29 U.S.C. § 1399(b)(2)(A)(i) allows the employer to seek review of the schedule of payments; however, this dispute also falls under § 1401, the arbitration provision, as being within § 1381 through § 1399.

Possible Answers

1. The federal rules require only that the complaint make a "short and plain statement of the claim showing that the pleader is entitled to relief." Fed. R. Civ. P. 8(a)(2). The Supreme Court has interpreted that phrase to mean the complaint must provide the defendant with "fair notice of what the plaintiff's claim is and the grounds upon which it rests," <u>Conley v. Gibson</u>, 355 U.S. 41, 47 (1957). The Third Circuit court has taken a somewhat narrower view of what constitutes a valid complaint. <u>Rotolo v. Burough of Charleroi</u>, 532 F.2d 920 (3rd Cir. 1976).

2. Quasi-in-rem jurisdiction was first based on the conceptual basis of state sovereignty. The Supreme Court held that a state has sovereign power over property and persons within its borders, and over nothing outside of them. <u>Pennoyer v. Neff</u>, 95 U.S. 714 (1878). Thus a state could legitimately require a nonresident to come into the state to defend a cause of action, or forfeit his forum property. A

more recent Supreme Court ruling, Shaffer v. Heitner, 433 U.S. 186 (1977), held that all assertions of state court power must meet standards of due process as articulated in another Supreme Court case, International Shoe v. Washington, 326 U.S. 310 (1945).

3. The United States Code allows the employer to seek review of the schedule of payments. 29 U.S.C. § 1399(b)(2)(A)(i). However, this dispute also falls under Section 1401, the arbitration provision, as being within Section 1381 through Section 1399.

Excessive/Intrusive Quotations

> *After a legal writing seminar, an enlightened lawyer decided to rewrite his office forms and stock client letters in Plain English. Immediately a long-time client called, demanding of the secretary: "Why did you write this letter and pretend your boss wrote it?"*

Legal writing is filled with quoted material that can interrupt the flow of the text. Our legal system is built on *stare decisis* and depends on precedent, and the best means of invoking the proper precedent is to refer to it by case name (if it is familiar to the audience) or by a full citation. You need to tell the reader where your information came from: what rule supports your conclusion, what court ruled what way on a similar question. This need, however, often leads us into unacceptable prose by novice legal writers when they quote long, bulky opinions and statutes. Actually, many seasoned practitioners also use quotations too often. Some are rushed for time and, rather than paraphrasing, cut and paste long quotations; others are afraid to vary from "The Word" as the legislature or court created it.

Huge blocks of quoted information cannot logically address the writer's main point—a court originally wrote that language to address an earlier point of another case, and the legislature wrote the entire section to cover all the contingencies, only one of which is probably at issue in the case. If you include a long block quotation in a memorandum or brief, you cannot simultaneously quote and explain to the readers how all of its points fit together with your case. Either you have to explain all the connections before you add the block quotation (a rare strategy), or you have to conclude the long quotation with a belated explanation of all the connections. Neither strategy will create contented readers. Some writers attempt to pinpoint pertinent words within a block quotation by underlining that language. Logic indicates that if only the underlined language is important, it alone should be quoted.

Pros and cons of long block quotations

Pro:
- can fit the important language into a larger context
- are easy to find on the page
- stand out on the page
- can highlight extended controversial/colorful language, like an extended metaphor

Con
- are easily skipped by hurried readers
- can be difficult to integrate into a writer's textual point
- can introduce extraneous material and even contradict the writer's intended point
- can create a black, dense look to a document
- can be interpreted as sloppy writing
- require an especially strong introductory tag line and conclusion in the writer's text

- reproduce poorly written prose of the original writer whose point is useful but whose prose is deadly

Pros and cons of shorter word/phrase quotations

<u>Pro</u>:
- integrate more easily into the writer's text
- keep the readers' focus on the writer's text rather than on other cases
- allow a writer to keep that part of a holding that employs colorful and controversial language that readers could find persuasive

<u>Con</u>:
- if used out of context, can destroy credibility

Pros and cons of paraphrasing

<u>Pro</u>:
- most successfully integrates outside information into a writer's own text
- creates shorter, smoother documents

<u>Con</u>:
- requires the writer to be more sophisticated with, and take more care to provide, careful signals
- should not be used when the exact wording is in dispute
- can fail if signals indicating who said what are too weak for readers to follow
- can confuse readers if writer quotes more than one source within a sentence

Integrating quoted material

It is a sign of masterful writing when quotations are correctly integrated into the writer's text:

This case is distinguishable from <u>Sharp v. Broadway Nat'l Bank</u>, 33 Tex. Sup. Ct. J. 225 (Feb. 14, 1990), on which Appellant relies. In the instant case, Appellant had what he requested even before he asked for it in the interrogatory. In Sharp and in all other cases the undersigned has found regarding the "good cause" issue, the discovery in question had to do with identity of a witness. Witness identity constitutes a necessary starting point for meaningful discovery, such as deposition of a witness, investigation of the witness' background, and questioning of other witnesses regarding anticipated testimony by the witness. In those types of cases, the Texas Supreme Court has been strict in limiting the trial court's discretion because "[t]he rules of discovery were changed to prevent trials by ambush and to ensure that fairness would prevail." Gutierrez v. Dallas Indep. Sch. Dist., 729 S.W.2d 691, 693 (Tex. 1987).

The paragraph above uses paraphrase (*Sharp*) and incorporates a portion of a direct quotation (*Gutierrez*), rather than full-text quotations of supporting material like the example below.

A Pennsylvania district court offered a strong reason for recognizing both the child and parent's claim to wrongful life:

> Society has an interest in ensuring that genetic testing is properly performed and interpreted. . . . The recognition of a cause of action for negligence in the performance of genetic testing would encourage the accurate performance of such testing by penalizing physicians who fail to observe customary standards of good medical practice.

Gildiner v. Thomas Jefferson Univ. Hosp., 451 F. Supp. 692, 696 (E.D. Pa. 1978).

In the *Gildiner* example the writer has done little to prepare readers for the content of the direct quotation; the "strong reason" is not explained outside of the quotation, which means the reader either reads the quotation carefully or loses the point. Legal writers should not assume that their readers will bother reading the blocked material; the point needs to be spelled out succinctly before the quotation follows with its proof and documentation.

Practice with Paraphrasing and Quoting

Rewrite the following sentences so that they read smoothly and correctly, adding or removing punctuation as needed.

1. Scott Turow describes the second month of his first semester as one of acceptance. "For the most part, an atmosphere of modesty and bonhomie has taken over. We no longer see each other as the unknown objects on which all the splashy accolades and achievements were displayed like the tour decals on luggage." SCOTT TUROW, ONE L 111 (1977).

2. This case revolves around Rule 1.3 of the ABA's Model Rules of Professional Conduct.

> A lawyer shall act with reasonable diligence and promptness in representing a client.

In this case we have a lawyer who waited six years to ask for a continuance.

Possible Answers

1a. (*add a colon as a transition*) Scott Turow describes the second month of his first semester as one of acceptance: "For the most part, an atmosphere of modesty and bonhomie has taken over. We no longer see each other as the unknown objects on which all the splashy accolades and achievements were displayed like the tour decals on luggage." SCOTT TUROW, ONE L 111 (1977).

b. (*incorporate quotation; is this now too long*?) Scott Turow, describing the second month of his first semester as one of acceptance, said that "an atmosphere of modesty and bonhomie has taken over. We no longer see each other as the unknown objects on which all the splashy accolades and achievements were displayed like the tour decals on luggage." SCOTT TUROW, ONE L 111 (1977).

2a. (*add a colon as a transition*) This case, focusing on a lawyer who waited six years to ask for a continuance, revolves around Rule 1.3 of the ABA's Model Rules of Professional Conduct: "A lawyer shall act with reasonable diligence and promptness in representing a client."

b. (*integrate as a clause*) In this case we have a lawyer who waited six years to ask for a continuance. The ABA's Model Rule of Professional Conduct 1.3 controls, stating that "A lawyer shall act with reasonable diligence and promptness in representing a client."

Explain what is wrong with the quotation and paraphrasing in these examples.

1. Under Florida law, prejudgment interest is proper in a specific performance decree. Defendants rely on <u>Town of Longboat Key v. Carl E. Widell & Son</u>, 362 So. 2d 719 (Fla. Dist. Ct. App. 1978), to claim that when damages are not liquidated until time of judgment, the claim is one for unliquidated damages and prejudgment interest must be denied. As noted in <u>Hurley v. Slingerland</u>, 480 So. 2d 104, 107 (Fla. Dist. Ct. App. 1985), the Florida Supreme Court has discredited the test espoused in <u>Town of Longboat</u> by adopting the test that a claim becomes liquidated and susceptible of prejudgment interest <u>where the trial court's order fixes the amounts due as of specific dates</u>, citing <u>Argonaut Ins. Co. v. May Plumbing Co.</u>, 474 So. 2d 212 (Fla. 1985).

2. Colo. Rev. Stat. Ann. § 38-41-101 (West 1990) states that "Eighteen years of adverse possession of any land shall be conclusive evidence of absolute ownership."

Possible Answers

1. (*Three cases thrown together out of sequence and without logical connections.*) Under Florida law, prejudgment interest is proper in a specific performance decree. Defendants rely on <u>Town of Longboat Key v. Carl E. Widell & Son</u>, 362 So. 2d 719 (Fla. Dist. Ct. App. 1978), to claim that when damages are not liquidated until time of judgment, the claim is one for unliquidated damages and prejudgment interest must be denied. *[Placement of* Hurley *citation interrupts logic of argument.]* The Florida Supreme Court has discredited the test espoused in <u>Town of Longboat</u> by adopting the test that a claim becomes liquidated and susceptible of prejudgment interest where the trial court's order fixes the amounts due as of specific dates *[underlining for emphasis implies a direct quotation, but there are no quotation marks to signal a direct quotation]*, <u>Hurley v. Slingerland</u>, 480 So. 2d 104, 107 (Fla. Dist. Ct. App. 1985) (citing <u>Argonaut Ins. Co. v. May Plumbing Co.</u>, 474 So. 2d 212 (Fla. 1985)).

2. (*Citations are not text.*) Colorado law requires a specific number of years for absolute ownership: "Eighteen years of adverse possession of any land shall be conclusive evidence of absolute ownership." Colo. Rev. Stat. Ann. § 38-41-101 (West 1990).

Faulty Parallelism

Parallel ideas are often forcefully conveyed in parallel grammatical structures. Verbs can be parallel, as can nouns, adjectives—indeed, full sentences. When properly executed, parallel structures frequently produce persuasive, memorable prose.

Say that I was a drum major for justice. Say that I was a drum major for peace. That I was a drum major for righteousness. And all of the other shallow things will not matter. (*Martin Luther King, Jr.*)

Let us never negotiate out of fear. But let us never fear to negotiate. (*John F. Kennedy*)

Keep syntactically equal items parallel

A stylistic problem can arise when a writer sets up a syntax that requires equal elements but then introduces an incongruous element.

What are the rights of Chansco under the lease regarding access to the parking lot of the shopping center, its rights against all parties involved, and what remedies are available to Chansco?

Notice that "access" and "its rights" logically complete their introductory word "regarding." The third element, though, "what remedies," does not logically complete "regarding" and is not parallel to the first two elements.

Keep signals apparent

Occasionally writers lose parallelism because they begin a list of items with an introductory word or phrase that is later omitted from the other parallel words or phrases:

Thus, the court held that the complaint was not vague or conclusory and it was "adequate to give notice of the claims asserted."

The phrase "and it was" seems to begin a second independent clause. It does not. The writer intended the entire next phrase to be the second object of "held," so the phrase needs an introductory "that" to parallel the first one:

Thus, the court held **that** the complaint was not vague or conclusory and **that** it was "adequate to give notice of the claims asserted."

Occasionally parallelism is lost because the list of items begins not with an omitted word, like the example above, but with an inadvertent *repetition* of "that":

He said **that** because he was going to file before June **that** the statute of limitations would not have run.

Even a sentence containing a numbered list can be misunderstood if it is not grammatically parallel:

Other provisions of Section 6 provide (1) for the requisites of the application for a bondsman's license, (2) for an investigation and hearing by the board, and (3) its denial of the application or approval conditioned on the applicant's filing of the required security deposit.

The omitted "for" in part (3) of these provisions would have completed the grammatical parallel of prepositional phrases (*for* its denial). Similarly, a series of things should have the appropriate article or preposition either just once or before each item: "the plaintiff, the defendant, and the judge" or "the plaintiff, defendant, and judge."

Keep items following correlative conjunctions parallel

Another frequent error is created by incorrectly balanced correlative conjunctions:

either . . . or
neither . . . nor
both . . . and
not only . . . but also

The sentence parts that follow these conjunctions should be equivalent but are frequently misplaced and therefore place the emphasis on incorrect sentence parts.

> The policemen were looking **neither** for the waitress **nor** the donut-eater, but the two rushed outside to identify themselves. (*emphasizes for*)

> The policemen were looking **for neither** the waitress **nor** the donut-eater, but the two rushed outside to identify themselves.

> **Not only** was the freshman student afraid of the new professors **but also** his classmates. (*emphasizes was the freshman student*)

> The freshman student was afraid of **not only** the new professors **but also** his classmates.

Practice Structuring Parallel Sentences

Redo these sentences as necessary to create parallel items within them.

1. It is the type of bureaucratic abuse that, unless someone complains about it, that is going to continue.

2. The plaintiff must show:

(1) A reasonable probability that the parties would enter into a contractual relationship;
(2) That the defendant acted maliciously by intentionally preventing the relationship from occurring with the purpose of harming the plaintiff;
(3) The defendant was not privileged or justified; and
(4) Actual harm or damage occurred as a result of the interference.

Possible Answers

1. (*repeated "that"*) It is the type of bureaucratic abuse that, unless someone complains about it, is going to continue.

2. (*List after introductory tag not grammatically parallel. Introduction could include "that" or each part of list should begin with it.*) The plaintiff must show

(1) **that** there is a reasonable probability that the parties would enter into a contractual relationship;
(2) **that** the defendant acted maliciously by intentionally preventing the relationship from occurring with the purpose of harming the plaintiff;
(3) **that** the defendant was not privileged or justified; and
(4) **that** actual harm or damage occurred as a result of the interference.

Tabulate these sentences to check their parallelism.

1. However, worthless securities of an affiliated corporation give rise to an ordinary loss deduction if the taxpayer owns stock possessing at least 80 percent of the voting power of all classes of its stock and at least 80 percent of each class of its nonvoting stock is owned directly by the taxpayer and more than 90 percent of the aggregate of its gross receipts for all taxable years has been from sources other than royalties, rents, dividends, interest, annuities, and gains from sales of stock or securities.

2. Additionally, several specific issues are in question: whether the assertions contained in a letter dated July 19, 1989, from the TWC (attached as Exhibit "1") can be factual findings; whether the directives contained in the letter constitute an order; what standard of review will the courts apply to the administrative decision; and whether the Chronicle could take an affirmative action to initiate the administrative process,

such as seeking an advisory opinion or a declaratory judgment.

Possible Answers

1. *(**Excessive coordination** within a coordinated structure and thus **ambiguous parallelism**. The 80 percent clause may be recast as two parallel statements (1) and (2), thus establishing three parallel ideas. OR the second 80 percent clause may be subordinate to (1) but instead is signaling coordination.)*

However, worthless securities of an affiliated corporation give rise to an ordinary loss deduction if:

(1) the taxpayer owns stock possessing at least 80 percent of the voting power of all classes of its stock, and

(2) at least 80 percent of each class of its nonvoting stock is owned directly by the taxpayer, and

(3) more than 90 percent of the aggregate of its gross receipts for all taxable years has been from sources other than royalties, rents, dividends, interest, annuities, and gains from sales of stock or securities.

However, worthless securities of an affiliated corporation give rise to an ordinary loss deduction if:

(1) the taxpayer owns stock possessing at least 80 percent of the voting power of all classes of its stock and at least 80 percent of each class of its nonvoting stock is owned directly by the taxpayer, and

(2) more than 90 percent of the aggregate of its gross receipts for all taxable years has been from sources other than royalties, rent, dividends, interest, annuities, and gains from sales of stock or securities.

2. *(introductory adverb switched from "whether" to "what" mid-series; need to remain consistent.)*

Additionally, several specific issues are in question:

(1) **whether** the assertions contained in a letter dated July 19, 1989, from the TWC (attached as Exhibit "1") can be factual findings;

(2) **whether** the directives contained in the letter constitute an order; and

(3) **whether** the Chronicle could take an affirmative action to initiate the administrative process, such as seeking an advisory opinion or a declaratory judgment.

A fourth issue is which standard of review the courts will apply to the administrative decision.

Conclusion

When you edit your draft, first examine the organization with its set-up and devices you have added that highlight your organizational pattern. Then scrutinize your sentence-level prose for long tangles that distort meaning. Pay particular attention to sentence length and order, to passives and left-handed sentences, and to the placement of citations. Before putting down your red pen, look once again for sentence elements you meant to parallel. Editing sentences not only will tighten them individually but will help reduce the overall length of your draft.

ADDITIONAL EXERCISES
(See Possible Answers in Appendix at page 180.)

I. Practice with Passives and Ambiguity

Rewrite the following sentences with active verbs that eliminate any ambiguity.

1. Since defendant RAVENSWOOD may be entitled to qualified immunity from a 28 U.S.C. § 1983 civil action, it must be determined whether defendant RAVENSWOOD's conduct violated any clearly established statutory or constitutional right.

2. It was thus impossible to determine if the conduct was protected by the first amendment, and under the <u>Nearich</u> test, the allegations were insufficient.

II. Practice with Long Sentences

Break the following sentences into manageable units with either tabulation, punctuation, or separate sentences. You may also add signposts and move subjects closer to their verbs, verbs closer to their objects.

1. In this connection, Plaintiff will show that the design and manufacture of the brakes and brake adjusters of the trucks in question were within the exclusive control of Defendants, that Plaintiff had no means of ascertaining the method or manner in which the product was designed and manufactured, and that the product came into Plaintiff's possession in the same condition it was in when it left the control of Defendants.

2. Defendants Rawdon Crawley, Pitt, and Sedley d/b/a Vanity Plaza Shopping Center with knowledge that Plaintiff was using the common areas of the Vanity Plaza Shopping Center intentionally and willfully entered into a contract for sale which interfered with the lease contract held by the Plaintiff in that no reservation of the Plaintiff's access rights to the common areas of the Vanity Plaza Shopping Center were protected and, therefore, causing the breach of Plaintiff's contract with Defendants Sharp and Vexating Properties Investment, Inc.

Find the verbs in the following sentences: How can they be moved so that readers can more easily find the subject/verb relationship? Can any of the sentences be broken into two sentences?

1. However, this Court's statement in the earlier order that it had received the Defendant's Reply which contained the first fraud on the court argument is certainly some indication that it

was considered, and the Defendant's assertions that "nothing could be further from the truth" and that Company's statements were "absolutely false" are sensational distortions at best.

2. Callins' assertions that jurors felt compelled to sentence him to death for the capital murder because they had not been aware during the first punishment hearing that they would also be sentencing him for capital murder, and they had assessed punishment for the robberies at life imprisonment was resolved against him as a factual matter at the hearing on his motion for a new trial.

Evaluate the length of the following sentence and either (1) justify leaving it at its current length or (2) choose one of the following methods to create a more understandable sentence: break into more than one sentence, punctuate for clarity, add signposts, reposition subject and verb closer together, tabulate.

State Insurance Code Annotated Article 21.12 § 3(c) requires the State Treasurer to hold the deposit exclusively for the protection of any "customer" obtaining a final judgment against the corporate Local Recording Agent and allows the withdrawal of a corporate Local Recording Agent financial responsibility deposit only upon an affirmative showing that it has withdrawn from business and has no unsecured liabilities outstanding, or that the corporation can prove financial responsibility by furnishing an errors and omission insurance policy or by posting a bond.

III. Practice Reorganizing Left-Handed Sentences

Flip-flop the following left-handed introductions or break the sentences in two.

1. In an action by a homeowner against a furnace seller who negligently installed the furnace resulting in a fire that destroyed the home and contents, the court of appeals held that mental distress was not a proper element for recovery.

2. In the event Landlord cannot obtain assurances satisfactory to Landlord that such separate rendition will not cause additional roll back taxes on the land owned by Landlord adjacent to the Leased Premises which is presently taxed on its agricultural value, then this lease shall be void and of no force or effect.

IV. Practice Placing Citations

Move or change the following citations so that they follow proper form and so that the text of the sentence outweighs the citation.

1. The general rule as discussed in <u>Anderson v. McBurney</u>, 467 N.W.2d 158, 160 (Wis. Ct. App. 1991); <u>Brown v. LaChance</u>, 477 N.W.2d 296, 300 (Wis. Ct. App. 1991), is that an attorney cannot be held liable to third parties for acts committed within the scope of attorney-client relationship, absent fraud or negligence in the drafting of an estate planning document. This exception has been narrowly construed by the courts of Wisconsin, which have held it valid in a limited context.

2. Plaintiffs misconstrue the holdings of <u>Stewart v. Rudner</u>, 84 N.W.2d 816 (Mich. 1957), <u>Avery v. Arnold Home, Inc.</u>, 169 N.W.2d 135, 137 (Mich. Ct. App. 1969), and <u>Allinger v. Kell</u>, 302 N.W.2d 576, 581 (Mich. Ct. App. 1981), in an attempt to establish that commercial contracts can also be personal in nature.

V. Practice with Paraphrasing and Quoting

Explain what is wrong with the quotation and paraphrasing in these examples.

1. "A person having .10% alcohol concentration is intoxicated per se." <u>Reardon v. State</u>, 695 S.W.2d 331, 333 (Tex. App.—Houston [1st Dist.] 1985, no writ).

Intoxication as defined by Article 6701-1(a)(2) means:

(A) not having the normal use of mental or physical faculties by reason of the introduction of alcohol, a controlled substance, a drug, or a combination of two or more of those substances into the body; or (B) having an alcohol concentration of .10% or more.

TEX. REV. CIV. STAT. ANN. art. 6701-(1)(a)(2) (Vernon Supp. 1985).

"The definition of 'intoxication' in Article 6701-1(a)(2)(b) does not give rise to any presumption of intoxication; an alcohol concentration of 0.10% constitutes intoxication standing alone." Reinsmith v. State, 703 S.W.2d 315, 316 (Tex. App.—Houston [14th Dist.] 1985, no writ). Article 6701-1(a)(2)(b) prohibits the operation of an automobile while a person has an alcohol concentration of 0.10% or more, regardless of the level of bodily impairment. Reardon, 695 S.W.2d at 333.

2. Writing about the Statement of Facts, Professor Karl Llewellyn concludes "It is a question of making the facts talk."

3. This obligation is not dependent upon Border's intention to submit to arbitration, but rather is imposed on the [c]orporation under the [statute]. ILGWU Nat'l Retirement Fund v. Levy Bros. Frocks, 846 F.2d 859, 885 (2d Cir. 1988); Teamsters Pension Trust Fund v. Allyn Transp. Co., 832 F.2d 502 (9th Cir. 1987).

VI. Practice Constructing Parallel Sentences

Redo these sentences as necessary to create parallel items within them.

1. Alternatively, plaintiff has not proved the necessary elements to prevail on the charge of intentional misrepresentation which are: (1) a material misrepresentation; (2) that is false; (3) the speaker knew it was false; (4) the statement was made with the intention that the plaintiff rely on it; (5) the

plaintiff relied on the misrepresentation; and (6) suffered injury.

2. Other provisions of section 6 provide for the requisites of the application for a bondsman's license, for an investigation and hearing by the board, and its denial of the application or approval conditioned on the applicant's filing of the required security deposits.

Tabulate this sentence to check parallelism.

3. If the list that follows the colon makes up an integral part of the introductory sentence, writers should remember to indent all of each item and to number each item, to begin each item with a lowercase letter, to end each item except the last with a semicolon, to use a semicolon and "and" or "or" on the next-to-last item, and to conclude the last item with a period unless the list does not conclude the sentence.

CHAPTER 3

Choosing Words with Style

> *Dan Quayle explaining what he said the night he was chosen George Bush's running mate: "I can't remember with any degree of recollection what I said."*

Precise word choice and strategic word placement can mean the difference between success and failure. To help you increase and hone your vocabulary, this chapter will highlight six common problems with words that cause substantive ambiguity:

1. jargon
2. wordiness
3. pronoun antecedents
4. noun strings and nominalizations
5. treacherous placement
6. gender-based language

Jargon

> *A lawyer is one who would trim*
> *From the language all words that are slim;*
> > *To "he died after her"*
> > *He will always prefer*
> *To aver that "she pre-deceased him."*

> —*unpublished limerick by Laurence Perrine, Professor of English Emeritus, SMU, Dallas*

Every profession has its share of *jargon*, that specialized vocabulary used within a group with common backgrounds or interests to save time and to imply an insider's connection. Newspaper editors "put the issue to bed," and students sign up for classes on "M-W-F or T-T." These jargon expressions communicate effectively to everyone within that group but baffle those outside it.

Terms of art, on the other hand, are a legal shorthand to summarize the underlying concepts. Attorneys depend on terms of art for daily communication among themselves: *dictum, garnishment, fee simple*. Readers untrained in the law cannot be expected to understand these terms, and, interestingly, many specialized words within one area of law confuse even other lawyers—car insurance policies can bewilder antitrust lawyers.

Legal writers inadvertently slip these specialized words and phrases into documents for laymen because they assume everyone else knows them also. Jargon, then, is a matter of *audience*. The needs of your audience must be met in each choice of word, just as they were met within your organizational choices. (*See* Chapter 1.)

To eliminate words that are jargon even to a legal audience, learn to identify and weed out *archaic legalisms*, for example, words with plain English equivalents:

Archaic legalism	*Plain English*
aforesaid	previous
forthwith	immediately
henceforth	from now on
herein	in this document
hereinafter	after this
thenceforth	after
thereafter	after that, accordingly
therein	in
theretofore	up to that time
hitherto	before
viz.	that is, for example
whence	from what place, source
whereby	through, in accordance
said	the, that
whilst	during

Additionally, be suspicious of *coupled synonyms*, which were useful hundreds of years ago when three languages (French, Latin, and versions of Old English) were used simultaneously on one English island:

acknowledge and confess	act and deed
aid and abet	annul and set aside
authorize and empower	absolutely and completely
covenant and surmise	deem and consider
covenant and agree	each and every
due and payable	each and all
excess and unnecessary	false and untrue
final and conclusive	full and complete
fit and proper	have and hold
for and in consideration of	force and effect
fraud and deceit	in truth and in fact
in my stead and place	from and after
free and unfettered	let or hindrance
for and during	for and in consideration of
give, devise, and bequeath	keep and maintain

last will and testament	truth and veracity
lot, tract, or parcel of land	modified or changed
null, void, and of no effect	order and direct
ordered, judged, and decreed	save and except
type and kind	void and of no effect

Although not all of these couplets are redundant,[1] fortunately most can be narrowed to one word.

Finally, new writers can be sensitive to *overused* legal phrases that are a part of jargon, including "in this instant case," "the case at bar," "the issue of whether," "one must prove," "the court below," "the said party," and "one must set out." Replacing them with the case name, the parties' names, and more specific pronouns will keep your prose specific and sharp.

Practice Finding Jargon

Find common terminology and shorter phrases to replace the following jargon.

1. TO THE HONORABLE JUDGE OF SAID COURT:
NOW COME defendants in the above styled and numbered cause and file this their Motion for Directed Verdict, and request that the court direct the jury to return a verdict in this cause and in support would show as follows: . . .

2. The instant plaintiff can argue . . .

---

1.   A commonsense warning: Be careful when you edit that you are not tossing out necessary legal terms. For instance, "ready, willing, and able" are not legally redundant. Someone could be *willing* to share a document but not *ready* because the material has not been produced. Similarly, for years the law divided property into land (real) and other property. Testators were required to both *bequeath* other property and *devise* real property. The words were not redundant because they referred to two separate means of disposing of property. Many states today no longer require the distinction, but it is important to beginning legal writers and editors that they understand the reason behind the legal terminology before they attempt to edit it for clarity and concision. *See* Terri LeClercq, *Jargon 2: Just When You Thought It Was Safe* . . . , 48 TEX. B.J. 852 (1985) (comparison of "fraud" and "deceit").

Possible Answers

1. TO THE HONORABLE JUDGE:
Defendants file this Motion for Directed Verdict and request that the court direct the jury to return a verdict. In support, Defendants offer the following: . . .

2. **Plaintiff Jones** can argue . . .

Decide which of the following sentences is appropriate for a legal audience but not a common readership.

1. Attached hereto is a genuine and authentic copy of the Promissory Note.
    Legal only _____   Common readership _____

2. In truth and in fact we order, judge, and decree this decision, save and except the plaintiff finds additional means to extract information from the defendant.
    Legal only _____   Common readership _____

3. The proceeds of such sale are to be distributed first, as reimbursement for expenses incurred in connection with such sale; second, to pay the unpaid principal amount of all certificates, plus accrued interest thereon; and third, to Black & Decker or its subsidiary/Lessee (as agreed upon between themselves).
    Legal only _____   Common readership _____

4. He also alleges violation of certain state law claims, to wit: fraud, breach of contract, and misrepresentation.
    Legal only _____   Common readership _____

Possible Answers

Jargon is highlighted:

1. Attached **hereto** is a **genuine and authentic** copy of the Promissory Note. *(Legal only)*

2. **In truth and in fact** we order, **judge, and decree** this decision, **save and except** the plaintiff finds additional means to extract information from the defendant. *(Legal only)*

3. The proceeds of **such** sale are to be distributed first, as reimbursement for expenses incurred in connection with **such** sale; second, to pay the unpaid principal amount of all certificates, plus accrued interest **thereon**; and third, to Black & Decker or its subsidiary/Lessee (as agreed upon between themselves). *(Common readership; business language plus legal "such" and "thereon")*

4. He also alleges violation of certain state law claims, **to wit**: **fraud, breach of contract**, and **misrepresentation**. *(Both legal and common readership. "To wit" is archaic, and the three claims encompass legal concepts. Common readers might understand the general claims but not the concepts.)*

Wordiness

> *Take the sentence, "The sky is blue." No junior associate would be so naive as to think this proposition could pass muster in a big firm. . . . [H]e knows enough to say, "The sky is generally blue." Better yet, "The sky generally appears to be blue." A senior associate seeing this sentence might . . . say: "In some parts of the world, what is generally thought of as the sky sometimes appears to be blue."*
> —Dan White, The Official Lawyer's Handbook 177 (1983)

Legal documents frequently read as if the office copier has accidentally repeated a page, or as if the personal computer has mistakenly duplicated the previous paragraph. Here are a few causes of the perpetual wordiness of legal writing:

1. unnecessary prepositions
2. passives
3. unnecessary relative pronouns
4. throat-clearers
5. unnecessary modification
6. redundancy

Because repetition results in lengthy documents and uninteresting reading, focus on your drafts with a critical eye. If you can cut a fourth out of your draft, it will deliver its message more forcefully.

Omit unnecessary prepositions

She consulted **with** her attorney **in regard to** her inheritance. *(10 words)*

REVISION

She consulted her attorney **about** her inheritance. *(7 words)*

The **language of the statute** will not explicitly tell you what the legislature intended. *(14 words)*

REVISION

The **statute's language** will not explicitly tell you the legislature's intention. *(11 words)*

Evaluate any unnecessary passive verbs

It was held by the court that the defendant was guilty of child abuse. *(14 words)*

REVISION

The court held the defendant guilty of child abuse. *(9 words)*

See also Chapter 2.

Omit unnecessary relative pronouns

He was the man **who** knocked on your door. *(9 words)*

REVISION

He knocked on your door. *(5 words)*

He said **that** it was a problem **that** he would look into. *(12 words)*

REVISION

He said he would look into the problem. *(8 words)*

There is no ironclad rule about the inclusion of "that," so common sense will have to tell you when you have used too many, or when you have lost the understanding that a relative pronoun provided.

Omit throat-clearers

Some writers need to warm up before delivering the pitch of the sentence and habitually begin sentences with "marshmallow" words just as a public speaker might say "uhmmm." Some examples:

obviously	clearly
manifestly	it would appear to be the case that
as a matter of fact	to tell the truth
it is obvious that	it is clear
case is when	situation is where
with all due respects	

Let's edit some phrases used not for transition but only as throat-clearers:

It is interesting that the child protection codes have changed so slowly. *(12 words)*

REVISION

The child protection codes have changed slowly. *(7 words)*

The **kind of** issue in these circumstances is probable cause. *(10 words)*

REVISION

The issue in these circumstances is probable cause. *(8 words)*

Writers should also be aware of unnecessary *expletives*, words we use to fill in slots. "There is," "there are," and "it is" are expletives. Many sentences beginning with expletives can be rewritten to vitalize the watered-down verbs hidden after the introduction:

There is no other method, except by deposition, in which Black can obtain this material. *(15 words)*

REVISION

Black cannot obtain this material except by deposition. *(8 words)*

It is important that fathers should continue to pay child support if the child chooses to attend college, even though the child is over the age of 18. *(28 words)*

REVISION

Fathers should continue to pay child support if the child chooses to attend college, even though the child is over 18. *(21 words)*

Not only are these revisions shorter, but their verbs also "act."

Some sentences may need to begin with "there is": "There is reason to worry today." It is clumsy and even wordier to edit this expletive into "A reason to worry today exists."

Avoid unnecessary modification

The second defendant is plainly and unequivocally innocent. *(8 words)*

REVISION

The second defendant is innocent. *(5 words)*

If the modification serves some tactical purpose, then it should be left in the text. If not, it should be deleted. The urge to modify can get writers into odd circumstances, perhaps even inadvertent oxymorons like "clearly indicate" and "allegedly injured." So check those modifiers before adding them to your descriptions.

Watch for redundancy

No one deliberately repeats words or ideas, but inadvertently you might express the same idea twice if you don't edit:

alleged suspect	irregardless *(not a word)*
consensus of opinion	next subsequent
free gift	personal (or honest) opinion
rather (or most) unique	reason is because
the said party	single most
whether or not[2]	

---

2. "Whether or not" is usually, but not always, redundant:

We do not know **whether or not** the executive summary will bring you immediate benefits. *(unnecessary "or not")*

But like most "rules," this one does not cover all possibilities:

Agency fees are collected to defray expenses of the activities of the union, expenses that benefit all members of the collective bargaining unit, **whether union members or not.**

Here the "or not" is syntactically necessary to complete the thought.

Sophisticated writers also avoid common redundancies like "co-conspirator" (why is "co" necessary?) and "reiterate" ("iterate" means to repeat; "reiterate" must mean repeat repeatedly). A writer who doesn't double-check could allow a slip like the following, to the amusement of readers:

> The **holdings** in <u>State v. Walker</u>, 441 S.W.2d 168 (Tex. 1969), and <u>State v. Schaffer</u>, 530 S.W.2d 813 (Tex. 1975), **hold** that new dissimilar construction bears doubtful relevance to the market value of condemned property.

Practice Eliminating Extra Words

> *A speaker should cultivate brevity*
> *With a suitable leaven of levity.*
> *In short, be terse,*
> *For nothing is worse*
> *Than interminable verbal longevity.*
> —James C. Humes, Podium Humor 52 (1975)

Which of these phrases can be shortened and yet not substantially changed?

1. for the purpose of evaluating

2. totally destroyed

3. future plans

4. went on to say that

5. false misrepresentation

6. mutual agreement

Possible Answers

All could be shortened without substantive changes.

Eliminate the unnecessary *prepositions* from the following sentences.

1. The obligation of the teacher may have existed in a moral way, but not in a legal way.

2. The Idaho court is likely to apply the traditional requirement that there must be an accompanying physical injury for the court to allow recovery for negligent infliction of emotional distress.

3. At a hearing on a request for a temporary injunction, the only question before the trial court is whether the applicant is entitled to preservation of the status quo of the subject matter of the suit pending a final trial of the case on the merits.

Possible Answers

1. The teacher's obligation may have been moral, but not legal.

2. The Idaho court is likely to apply the traditional requirement that there must be an accompanying physical injury if the plaintiff is to recover for negligent infliction of emotional distress.

3. At a temporary injunction hearing, the only question before the trial court is whether the applicant is entitled to preservation of the status quo of the subject matter of the suit, pending the case's final trial on the merits.

Review the following sentences for the use, abuse, omission, or overuse of "that." Which sentences would you change, and why?

1. Plaintiff specifically objects to Defendant's request for appraisal reports prepared for the State Department of High

ways and Public Transportation that cover parcels that are not comparable to the parcel that is the subject matter of this lawsuit.

2. The main reason that the strikers did not cross the picket lines was that they wanted to show solidarity to the management.

3. In <u>Halbert</u>, the definition of "hospital" was essentially the same as provided in our policy. The court found that because the psychiatric hospital did not provide major surgical facilities, diagnostic facilities, or X-ray equipment, that it did not fall within the definition of "hospital" provided for in the insurance policy.

Possible Answers

1. *(change—too many "that"s:)* Plaintiff specifically objects to Defendant's request for appraisal reports prepared for the State Department of Highways and Public Transportation. These reports cover parcels not comparable to the parcel that is the subject matter of this lawsuit.

2. *(change—wordy:)* The strikers did not cross the picket lines because they wanted to show solidarity to the management.

3. *(change—repeated "that":)* In <u>Halbert</u>, the definition of "hospital" was essentially the same as our policy provides. The court found that because the psychiatric hospital did not provide major surgical facilities, diagnostic facilities, or X-ray equipment, it did not fall within the definition of "hospital" provided for in the insurance policy.

Pronoun Antecedents

> *I know you lawyers can, with ease,*
> *Twist words and meanings as you please;*
> *That language, by your skill made pliant,*
> *Will bend to favour ev'ry client[.]*
> —2 John Gay, The Dog and the Fox, in *Fables 1 (1738)*

If a sentence has more than one possible antecedent (noun) or the antecedent is left unstated, its orphaned pronoun leaves the reader wondering who did what with (or to) whom.

Multiple antecedents

Sentences with more than one noun can contain multiple possible antecedents for a pronoun. If the pronoun is nearer one of the nouns, chances of confusion are narrowed but not eliminated. But once the pronoun is separated from its noun by intruding verbs and phrases, confusion is inevitable.

> Because he was screaming abuses, the defendant ordered the police officer to arrest the man. *(Who was screaming: The defendant? The police officer? The man? We need the pronoun attached to one of the nouns for clarity.)*

Sometimes it is difficult for writers to recognize that they have created several antecedents for a pronoun. Recently, for instance, the Texas Employment Commission had to change its standard instructions to its hearing examiners because readers insisted they did not know who or what was being excluded from the hearing:

> This hearing will be conducted via a telephone conference call by the hearing officer listed above. The par-

ties are advised that they should immediately mail any documents they intend to rely upon as evidence in the hearing to the hearing officer and the other party at the addresses listed above. Failure to provide the other party with a copy of the document(s) may result in **their exclusion** from the hearing.

The Commission's executives had to edit the last sentence to read "Failure may result in the **document's exclusion** from the hearing." Both parties were thus allowed to remain in the hearing, despite any untimely documentation.

Relative and demonstrative pronouns

Unstated or "understood" antecedents also create trouble for legal writers using relative pronouns (noun substitutes *who, whom, whose, that, which, what, whoever, whomever, whichever,* and *whatever,* but especially *that* and *which*) and demonstrative pronouns (*this, that, these,* and *those* used to point out). A typical problem with demonstrative pronouns is the ambiguity highlighted below:

> Under the scope of discovery in Rule 26(b)(3), "the court shall protect against disclosure of any mental impressions, conclusions, opinions, or legal theories of an attorney." **This** would seem to disallow interrogatory number two.

One technique for avoiding these ambiguous demonstrative pronouns is to follow *this, that,* and *which* with concrete nouns:

> **This rule** disallows interrogatory number two.

In a contract or agreement, the ambiguous pronoun could leave your client wide open to unfortunate interpretations.

Adonis' contacts with New York were not "irregular or casual," **which** resulted in the protection of New York's laws being afforded to him. *(What resulted in New York's protection: the contacts or the fact that the contacts were not irregular or casual?)*

REVISIONS

Adonis' contacts with New York were not "irregular or casual"; therefore, he is protected by New York's laws.

Adonis' contacts with New York, which resulted in his being protected by New York's laws, were not "irregular or casual."

Practice Spotting Ambiguous Pronouns

Rewrite the following sentences, replacing the ambiguous pronouns and limiting a pronoun's referents.

1. The question is whether Smith informed others of the defect in the tank design and if this caused the loss of benefits Boeing expected from these companies.

2. If there is a case on point with a similar fact situation and you are discussing an issue that calls for argument, this will give more weight to your argument.

3. Thus, the "IV-D" plan requires that the State pursue reimbursement from absent parents for the public assistance provided for the necessary support of their children. The distribution of collections adheres to that.

Possible Answers

1. The question is whether Smith informed others of the defect in the tank design and if their **knowing about the defect** caused the loss of benefits Boeing expected from these companies.

The question**s are** whether Smith informed others of the defect in the tank design, **and whether others knowing it** caused the loss of benefits Boeing expected from these companies.

2. If a case on point has a similar fact situation and you are discussing an issue that calls for argument, **the similar facts** will give more weight to your argument.

3. Thus, the "IV-D" plan requires that the State pursue reimbursement from absent parents for the public assistance provided for the necessary support of their children. The distribution of collections adheres to that **requirement**.

Correct the following sentence, which contains illogically embedded "which" clauses.

Buyers and Sellers have entered into an Earnest Money Contract-Commercial Unimproved Property ("Earnest Money Contract") effective as of December 18, 1990, for the purchase of certain property ("Property"), which Property is more fully described in the Earnest Money Contract.

Possible Answer

Buyers and Sellers have entered into an Earnest Money Contract-Commercial Unimproved Property ("Earnest Money Contract") effective as of December 18, 1990, for the purchase of certain property ("Property"). **This Property** is more fully described in the Earnest Money Contract.

Noun Strings and Nominalizations

> *Cleansed of words without reason, much of the language of the law need not be peculiar at all. And better for it.*
> —David Mellinkoff, The Language of the Law 454 (1963)

Noun strings are primary culprits in making legal writing

dense and difficult to understand. In a noun string, a succession of nouns modify each other; thus, each preceding noun functions as an adjective that modifies the last noun:

The	*bank's*	*contract*	*credit*	*review*	*service*
	modifier	*modifier*	*modifier*	*modifier*	*noun*

Until readers locate that final noun, they must assume that each noun functions as a noun but then later reprocess those previous nouns into adjectives.

Each area of the law has particular noun strings that are shorthand within that particular area, but the strings baffle outside readers. Look, for instance, at the title of a recent law review article: *Copyright Law: Integrating Successive Filtering into the Bifurcated Substantial Similarity Inquiry in Software Copyright Infringement Cases.* Is the author saying that the similarity inquiry is bifurcated-substantial or is the author describing a substantial-similarity inquiry? Probably even a bifurcated attorney won't know.

Noun strings camouflage the logical relationship between the nouns, and between the nouns and any adjective that may precede them.

qualified scholarship funding bonds

- qualified-scholarship?
- qualified scholarship-funding?

intrusive pretrial discovery methods

- intrusive-pretrial discovery methods?
- intrusive pretrial-discovery methods?

Rather than force the reader to do all the work, a writer has the option of either adding a hyphen or breaking up the string.

Solutions to noun strings

The first solution to noun strings is the *hyphen*. It connects two or more of the adjectives:

low-interest real estate loans
one-time tax write off

A second solution to noun strings is to *unstring them* and make the nouns' relationship accessible to the reader:

a gross receipt sales tax

- a gross-receipt sales tax
- a sales tax on gross receipts

new financial institutions franchises

- new financial-institutions franchises
- franchises for new financial institutions

Another stylistic problem is created by *nominalizations*. Nominalizing nouns and verbs is the result of switching base verbs and concrete nouns into unnecessarily multisyllabic words with Latinate suffixes and prefixes such as *-ize, -osity, -ate, -ability, -tion, -ancy, -ion, -al, -ence, -ive, -ment, de-,* and *mis-* (examples: investig**ation**, necess**itate**, intellig**ence**, **mis**appropriate).

(*original*) We made an investigation before we deposed the witness.
(*concrete*) We investigated before deposing the witness.

(*original*) The last memorandum necessitated our calling a firm-wide meeting.
(*concrete*) Because of the last memorandum, we had to call a firm-wide meeting.
(*concrete*) We called a meeting because the last memorandum required it.

Although grammatically correct, nominalizations dilute a sentence by implying, rather than stating, the logical who/what relationships in the sentence.

Watch for these nouns created from verbs:

determination from *to determine*
resolution from *to resolve*
utilization from *to use*
reinforcement from *to enforce*
the addition of from *to add*
assumption from *to assume*
continuation from *to continue*

Also watch for nouns created from adjectives (that were once verbs):

enforceability from *enforceable* from *enforce*
applicability from *applicable* from *apply*
specificity from *specific* from *specify*

Reading page after page of nominalizations, audiences may give up in exhaustion because they have to mentally unravel both the true noun and its hidden relationship to other parts of the sentence. A good check for your draft is to read each sentence separately, applying the "who did what to whom?" test.

> The formal consultive relationship will focus on the insights gained from current cost accounting and annuity depreciation for enhanced security performance measurement and evaluation.

In the above example, who/what is going to focus on insights, and what does that mean? "Performance," "measurement," and "evaluation" each have a hidden verb that could be revived and turned into actions that readers could follow:

We can measure and evaluate how the security performs.

Practice Finding Noun Strings

Unravel these strings, separating nouns and adding connecting words or hyphens as necessary. Which terms are so ambiguous that the writer's intent cannot be determined?

1. cash flow calculation expense amounts

2. funded welfare insurance programs

3. the bank's contract credit review service

Possible Answers

1. cash-flow calculation expense-amounts (*ambiguous to general reader; the phrase's author insists this solution represents the intended relationship*)

2. funded welfare-insurance programs

3. the bank's review service for contract credit

Practice Finding Nominalizations

Replace nominalizations with strong verbs and adjectives.

1. The reason a five-year lease diminishes Black & Decker's indicia of ownership with respect to the Equipment is that a five-year lease allows the lessor to exercise dominion and control (i.e., manifestation of ownership) over the Equipment upon its surrender at the expiration of the lease term.

2. Thank you for allowing our firm to make our presentation of international issues related to your business.

Possible Answers

1. (*nominalizations in the original identified in bold:*) The reason a five-year lease diminishes Black & Decker's indicia of ownership with respect to the Equipment is that a five-year lease allows the lessor to exercise dominion and control (i.e., **manifestation** of ownership) over the Equipment upon **its surrender** at the **expiration** of the lease term.

(*correction:*) A five-year lease diminishes Black & Decker's indicia of ownership over the Equipment because a five-year lease allows the lessor dominion and control (i.e., **to manifest** ownership) over the Equipment when the owner **surrenders** it when the lease **expires.**

2. (*nominalizations in the original identified in bold:*) Thank you for allowing our firm **to make our presentation** of international issues related to your business.

(*correction:*) Thank you for allowing our firm **to present** the international issues related to your business.

Treacherous Placement

> *They fired their summer clerk yesterday.*
> *Only they fired their summer clerk yesterday.*
> *They only fired their summer clerk yesterday.*
> *They fired only their summer clerk yesterday.*
> *They fired their only summer clerk yesterday.*
> *They fired their summer-only clerk yesterday.*
> *They fired their summer clerk only yesterday.*

A few words in the English language create more chaos than all the others added together. "Only" slips in and out of sentences and destroys meaning. Legal writers believe the placement of "however" is controversial. Undoubtedly the most pernicious misplacement is the positioning of modifiers, which is the "Doctrine of the Last Antecedent" in legal writing.

"Only"

"Only" modifies or emphasizes the word immediately following it. (See the summer clerk examples above.) For example, when "only" splits the commonplace medical direction "for occasional use only as directed," the "only" becomes a "squinting modifier" that can confuse average medicine-takers: They may believe the medicine is intended for occasional use only. (*For occasional use only. As directed.*) Or they may interpret the instruction to mean that the medicine should be used only as directed. (*For occasional use. Only as directed.*) Perhaps these directions will end up before a court some day, with a patient insisting he had followed directions and a medicine company arguing that the instructions *clearly* support its interpretation.

"However"

Legal writers can place the introductory adverb, "however," with the same freedom as "nevertheless," "moreover," and so on.[3] The placement of "however" is a stylistic decision, and writers have the option of choosing its placement so that it emphasizes the intended contrast:

> The world of the law is another world; **however**, the law thinks it's the whole world. JOHN MORTIMER, RUMPOLE OF THE BAILEY (1978).

---

3. When *The Elements of Style* hit the professional world with its collection of writing advice, many writers agreed with Strunk and White that "however" should not begin a sentence unless it means "in whatever way" or "to whatever extent"; e.g., "However you talk to him, he will still believe you are angry." WILLIAM STRUNK, JR. & E.B. WHITE, THE ELEMENTS OF STYLE 49 (3d ed. 1979). This suggestion can work for certain sentences, but it does not limit the placement of "however."

The world of the law is another world; the law, **however**, thinks it's the whole world.

The world of the law is another world; the law thinks, **however**, it's the whole world.

The world of the law is another world; the law thinks it's the whole world, **however**.

Each of these options emphasizes a different part of the saying; none is wrong, but some may be more effective than others. Choosing the location of your "however" will involve deciding where the word best suits your sentence's needs.

Doctrine of the last antecedent

A sentence containing a modifier with two or more nouns may force the writer to locate the modifier next to the antecedent noun and to hope it will not be confused for a modifier of each of the nouns:

I own an old tractor and car.

The tractor is definitely old; the car may also be old. "May be" is not concise enough for legal readers; precise modification is essential. Courts are forced to decide about contracts with modifiers floating among several nouns; similarly, lawyers argue endlessly over modifications in sections of statutes and codes.

Careful writers should evaluate each modifier within their documents to see if any modifying phrase could modify more than one noun. If the modifier is supposed to apply to all of the antecedents, then writers should either repeat the modifier for each antecedent or place a comma between the last antecedent and the phrase. The comma can signal universal application:

The candidate must pass the written test and the durability test, within one week before beginning work. *(must do both)*

Within one week of beginning work, the candidate must pass the written test and the durability test. *(must do both)*

If you intend to limit the modifier to only one noun within the sentence, then break the sentence in two or add additional limitations to the antecedents:

The candidate must pass the written test within one week before beginning work, and he should also pass the durability test.

The candidate must, within one week before beginning work, pass the written test. He also must pass the durability test.

References to this ambiguity in legal drafting were addressed by Jabez Southerland in 1891 in the "Doctrine of the Last Antecedent" rule.[4] Unfortunately, the rule has met with mixed success as a means of interpretation because so few people are

---

4.   JABEZ SOUTHERLAND, SOUTHERLAND ON STATUTORY CONSTRUCTION § 267 (1st ed. 1891):

> Referential and qualifying phrases, where no contrary intention appears, refer solely to the last antecedent. The last antecedent is the last word, phrase, or clause that can be made an antecedent without impairing the meaning of the sentence. This proviso usually is construed to apply to the provision or clause immediately preceding it. The rule is another aid to discovery of intent or meaning and is not inflexible and uniformly binding. Where the sense of the entire act requires that a qualifying word or phrase apply to several preceding or even succeeding sections, the word or phrase will not be restricted to its immediate antecedent.
>
> Evidence that a qualifying phrase is supposed to apply to all antecedents instead of only to the immediately preceding one may be found in the fact that it is separated from the antecedents by a comma.

aware of the punctuation clue. The best advice, obviously, is to avoid drafting any sentence in which the modifiers could be misunderstood.

Practice with Word Placement

Examine these sentences for their logic and emphasis.

1. Mr. Petty is neither expected to pay to testify as an expert witness in this action, nor does his opinion, report, or work product form the basis in either whole or in part of any experts who are to be called as witnesses.

2. Not only is this conclusion supported by the "facts and circumstances" test adopted by the Court of Appeals but also by the legislative change in the Business and Commercial Code.

3. You may call me at work, at the gym, or at home in the afternoon.

Possible Answers

1. **Neither is Mr. Petty** expected to pay to testify as an expert witness in this action, **nor does his opinion**, report, or work product form the basis **in either** whole or in part of any experts who are to be called as witnesses.

2. This conclusion is supported **not only by** the "facts and circumstances" test adopted by the Court of Appeals **but also by** the legislative change in the Business and Commercial Code.

3a. You may call me **in the afternoon** at work, at the gym, or at home.

b. You may call me at work, at the gym, or at home, **in the afternoon.**

Examine the placement of "only" plus "however" and other connecting adverbs in these sentences. If they are misplaced or ambiguous, correct them.

1. Article 2.11(B) only requires diligence to be used to locate the registered agent at the registered address.

2. He claims the psychiatrist, however, contradicted himself during the competency hearing by stating affirmatively that Porter was competent to stand trial.

Possible Answers

1. Article 2.11(B) requires **only** that diligence be used to locate the registered agent at the registered address.

2a. *(depends on context:)* He claims the psychiatrist contradicted himself during the competency hearing, **however**, by stating affirmatively that Porter was competent to stand trial.

b. **However**, he claims the psychiatrist contradicted himself during the competency hearing by stating affirmatively that Porter was competent to stand trial.

Gender-Based Language

> *An attorney worried all morning over the awkward options for beginning a letter to one female and four male bankers. Rather than the bulky "Dear Sirs and Madam," his solution was to drop the woman's name from the inside address list, address the letter "Dear Sirs," and add at the bottom of the letter, "c.c. Texanna McPhail."*

Once you accept the fact that the English language has a bias toward the male gender, you have taken the major step toward eliminating bias (fire*man*, *man*kind, an attorney should call *his* office). Nouns with "man" as a base have become a focal point for social criticism, so legal writers have to balance the precision of precedent against possible synonyms. Similarly, gender-based pronouns can perpetuate bias, so contemporary legal writers need to evaluate their subliminal impact. Perhaps, someday, someone will invent a new third-person pronoun with no gender implications. Right now, though, your client's contract or will is a poor place to engage in a personal war on sexism. When possible, legal stylists defer to the following alternatives to avoid the "he" limitations of the English language.

(1) Switch your sentence to the third-person plural where possible:

Everyone is expected to take his clients to lunch.

REVISIONS

All attorneys are expected to take their clients to lunch.

The partners expect all third-year associates to take their clients to lunch.

The third-person plural can create unnecessary ambiguity, so make sure both noun and pronoun are plural. Otherwise, you are creating yet another problem while trying to correct the problem of sexist language.

Each of the attorneys decided their Friday wardrobes should be casual.

This revision, substituting the plural "their" to avoid "his" or "her," produces confusion. "Each" is a singular noun that traditionally requires a singular pronoun.

REVISIONS

All of the attorneys decided their Friday wardrobes should be casual.

Each of the attorneys decided his or her Friday wardrobe should be casual.

(2) Drop the pronoun where possible: "The average prisoner calls his lawyer in the first hour of arrest" easily becomes "The average prisoner calls a lawyer in the first hour of arrest."

(3) Refer to people by occupation or qualification instead of gender.

Improvement in water quality in major cities is man's goal for the next decade.

REVISION

The voters' goal for the next decade is improvement in water quality in major cities.

Obviously, your context would present your cue for the shift.

(4) If the document is not long, you may find you can substitute she/he or he/she.[5]

---

5. Nonetheless, essayist Cyra McFadden has a point when complaining about an after-dinner speaker at a professional dinner:

> I heard a text replete with "he/she's" and "his/her's" read aloud for the first time. The hapless program female chairperson stuck with the job chose to render these orally as "he-slash-she" and "his-slash-her," turning the following day's schedule for conference participants into what sounded like a replay of the Manson killings.
>
> Redress may be due those of us who, though female, have answered to masculine referents all these years, but slashing is not the answer; violence never is. Perhaps we could right matters by using feminine forms as the generic for a few centuries, or simply agree on a per-woman lump-sum payment. . . . [D]efend it on any grounds you choose; the neutering of spoken and written English, with its attendant self-consciousness, remains ludicrous. In print, those "person" suffixes and "he/she's" jump out from the page, as distracting as a cloud of gnats, demanding that the reader note the writer's virtue. "Look what a nonsexist writer person I am, avoiding the use of masculine forms for the generic."

Cyra McFadden, *In Defense of Gender*, THE NEW YORK TIMES MAGAZINE, Aug. 2, 1981, at 9.

(5) Vary the document's pronouns from "he" to "she," if and only if the variation does not change the meaning of your document. You might, for instance, create a deliberate pronoun shift: "A professor normally instructs her classes three times a week." Be aware that few readers can follow a discussion in which "he" switches to "she" and back again within the same paragraph.

Practice with Gender-Based Language

What would you do about word choice in the following situations?

1. You are returning a business letter to a banker, who has signed an initial inquiry as "J.W. Smith." What is a proper salutation?

2. You are writing co-counsel to update them. You have three males and one female co-counsel. After listing them in the inside address lines, how do you address all of them on the salutation line?

3. In the preparation of tax advice to a group of sculptors, you need to refer to the artist who has traveling exhibitions, to the artist who uses a publicist, etc. How do you resolve the "he" or "she" controversy for the group-mailing advice letter?

4. As you prepare a brief for your client, you realize that she is an ardent feminist and that you have consistently used "he" as a generic to refer to "anyone under the law who . . . ."

Possible Answers

1. You might begin "Dear J.W. Smith" or you might call and ask for the full name.

2a. Dear Mr. Smith, Jones, and McMueller, and Ms. McCrary

b. Dear Counselors

3. You can use the third-person plural: **artists** who need to wrap **their** exhibitions . . . **artists** with individual **publicists**. . . .

4. Depending on your relationship with the client, you might

(1)   leave the specific court and legislative language as quoted but switch unnecessary masculine pronouns to the feminine,

(2)   add a cover letter explaining that legal convention will not allow you to change the pronouns, but you wish you could, or

(3)   discuss the options with her.

Conclusion

Responsibility for clear and concise language rests with each legal writer. Choosing, narrowing, and restricting words must always be done within the expectation of the audience and the presupposition it brings to that reading—never an easy task. But that task is the task of legal wordsmiths. Even those dedicated to precision can be tripped up by outside interpretation of familiar language.

Only by examining a contract or memorandum word for word, while considering each idea in relation to surrounding ideas, can the drafters anticipate any ensuing confusion. That's the role of an attorney: to satisfy the current needs of the drafters and the future needs of any possible audience. That ability cannot be achieved the day attorneys begin drafting a document: It has to be nurtured and developed through the investigation of words, the study of legal precedent and scholarship, and even the study of style in news magazines, political essays, novels, and poems.[6] Precise word choice is a lifetime pursuit with frustrations, plateaus, and delicious personal and professional rewards.

ADDITIONAL EXERCISES
(See Possible Answers in Appendix at page 186.)

I. Practice Finding Jargon

Find common terminology and shorter phrases to replace the following jargon.

1. This claim is contra to one of the most deeply held beliefs of our society.

2. Manufacturing will have the final say in the elongation of this time frame.

3. The lack of attendance has created the situation where we do not know the status of work items. Therefore, we cannot access our ability to accomplish the schedule.

4. Thank you for your anticipated assistance promoting resolution to these issues.

II. Practice Finding Noun Strings

Unravel these strings, separating nouns into prominent positions and adding connecting words or hyphens as necessary. Which terms are so ambiguous that the writer's intent cannot be determined?

---

6.   The craft behind a three-line haiku is a stellar example of concision:

While I turned my head
    that traveler I'd just passed . . .
melted into mist.

SHIKI, JAPANESE HAIKU (1956).

1. other local exchange companies' access service tariffs for switched transport per minute rates

2. parent company debt service requirements

3. well-established common law cause of action

4. state jeopardy diesel fuel tax assessments

5. the correct substantive evidence rule test

6. six-inch ~~thick~~ concrete pallets

7. certified return receipt postcard ~~receipt~~ of plaintiff's motion

III. Practice Eliminating Wordiness

Which of these phrases can be shortened?

1. deeply profound

2. tuna fish

3. in my heart I believe

4. my wife is unemployed for a living

5. the very first case filed

6. currently there are now five state laws

7. sudden emergency

8. honest opinion

9. next subsequent

10. in the near future

Eliminate the unnecessary *prepositions* from the following sentences.

1. This effort was made in a most casual way.

2. The grade was not a choice of the teaching assistant.

Eliminate any unnecessary words in the following sentences.

1. The Company's failure to purchase insurance breached the Dismantling Contract by failing to comply with the obligation imposed by Paragraph G.

2. The Commission went on to conclude that the plaintiff should not have been in court at all.

3. The purpose of this brief will be to examine the Equal Rights Amendment as a positive defense in an employment discrimination case.

4. The sales price would have been taxable whether or not the book was sold directly to the vendors or the end consumer.

5. It is important to note that the earlier discussion of the computation of time periods is relevant here. However, it must be noted that under one statutory interpretation, the ninety-day period is computed from the original due date.

6. After researching this issue, there appears to be no definitive line of demarcation in the determination of whether the proposed arrangement is a sale and leaseback or a financing arrangement for sales tax purposes.

IV. Practice Spotting Ambiguous Pronouns

Rewrite the following sentences, replacing the ambiguous pronouns and limiting a pronoun's referents.

1. It is well established that the design of roads and bridges is a discretionary function, and the State will not be liable for such decisions, which is consistent with cases that hold decisions made at the policy level instead of operational level are immune.

2. Caldwell did not cross-examine Hapless in the presence of the jury and now contends, as he did on direct appeal, that by not being able to go into Hapless' background, he was prevented from showing his bias or prejudice for testifying as he did, in violation of his Sixth Amendment right to confrontation.

3. In Veneer, the alleged tort-feasor would have been at a tactical disadvantage if the lawsuit were delayed by the injured party. This prompted the court to say that it would be in the interest of justice to permit it.

4. The municipality would have the information concerning the location of the arrest and the identity of the co-defendant policeman in its possession and the defendant could easily combine this information with the information contained in the complaint. It will probably provide a sufficiently specific factual basis for the time of the alleged violation, the place where it occurred, and those responsible.

5. The court in Matthews held that where "plain, adequate, and complete" relief is available, the aggrieved party "is left to that remedy in the state courts" unless a federal question is involved. 284 U.S. 526 (1927). Following the enactment of § 1341 in 1937, this theme was broadened by the United States Supreme Court.

Examine the placement of "only" plus "however" and other connecting adverbs in these sentences. If they are misplaced or ambiguous, correct them.

1. Success on the grounds of limitations can only be had if the court follows Wilson's lead and recognizes the appropriate statute of limitations is provided by the wrongful death statute.

2. In the event a lawsuit of either type could be successfully prosecuted, the courts would only prohibit non pari-mutuel racing at the track until registration can be completed.

3. First, the City asserts that a medical malpractice cause of action can only be proven by the testimony of an outside medical expert. The expert has, however, contradicted his own theory.

4. He wants to file in state court. However, it has only been two weeks since the case was dismissed from the federal court.

5. Agent further acknowledges that Owner will only accept financing of the sale through one of the four following methods.

CHAPTER 4

Punctuating with Style

> *Punctuation has long been considered the stronghold of inflexible and prescriptive rules. This tradition is unfortunate. To a great degree, punctuation is variable, flexible, and even imaginative.*
> —William D. Drake, The Way to Punctuate xii (1971)

When writers added punctuation to their written speeches in the third century B.C., they signaled places for speakers to pause. The different marks signaled the length of pause for the reader/speaker. Today's punctuation is governed by only a few rules (*see* Appendix at pages 139-142); most punctuation is optional and reflects the number and length of pauses writers want their readers to take.

To choose from several punctuation options, first decide what message you want to send your readers.

I. To make readers STOP COMPLETELY for a moment:

Use a period.

Periods generally signal the conclusion of a complete, independent clause, like this one. (Or incomplete, if informality is desired.)

II. To make readers STOP BUT IMMEDIATELY READ ON:

A. Use a semicolon.

The choice of a semicolon over a period is one of preference. Semicolons signal a pause weaker than a period but stronger than a comma. Look at the way a semicolon is constructed, with both a period ("stop") and a comma ("pause but go"). That is the double purpose of a semicolon.

> By the plain language of Rule 68, only the terms of the judgment finally obtained may be compared to the offer of judgment; non-judgment relief is not included.

B. Use a comma with the conjunction between two independent clauses.

A comma generally signals a short pause, and when coupled immediately with a conjunction, the comma invites a quick continuation for the eye.

> The bailiff asked the audience of the court to rise, and everyone stood together.

C. Use a colon.

A colon signals a pause stronger than a semicolon and suggests a more direct relationship between two ideas: It tells the reader that what follows will illustrate or amplify what has gone before.

> Benjamin Franklin saw a relationship between fish and visitors: They both stink after three days.

III. To ask readers to PAUSE or SLOW DOWN for a moment:

A. Use a comma.

(1) Writers need a comma after an introductory clause with its own subject and verb to warn readers that the main subject and verb are next.

> Because I could not stop for Death, He kindly stopped for me.

(2) Writers have an option of slowing readers down after a short introductory clause or phrase.

> By July 1990 he had turned in his resignation.
> By July 1990, he had turned in his resignation.

Inadequate punctuation of some short introductory phrases can confuse readers because they misread the complete sentence and then reread to separate the elements.

> In San Antonio jazz and mariachi bands vie for prominence.

In the above example, readers encounter four nouns before the main verb ("vie"); a comma after the introductory phrase "In San Antonio" would set the first noun apart from the two that act as adjectives before the sentence's main subject ("bands").

See if you can process this sentence the first time you read it:

> In each one word is missing.
>
> REVISION
>
> In each, one word is missing.

(3) Writers finishing one sentence but wanting to connect it to the next sentence through a conjunction (*and, or, nor, but, for, yet*) can slow legal readers down with a comma. In nontechnical writing, the comma between independent clauses is more of an option: "The boys screamed and their baby-sitter made them go to bed." Technical writers, including legal writers, add the comma between independent clauses to signal that the subject has changed from the first independent clause to the next.

> The plaintiff's car hit the newsstand and the driver behind him failed to stop.

In this example, readers assume the plaintiff's car hit the newsstand *and* the driver—until they find the second verb, "failed." Then they have to reread and reprocess.

> The comma is not always essential in all types of writing, but legal writers signal an impending new subject/verb with it.

(4) Similarly, legal writers can signal nonessential or explanatory information with a pair of commas.

> It is up to Congress, **not the courts,** to change the law.

> The new secretary, **however good she may be,** will have to be replaced by someone with seniority.

The commas mark the boundaries of the interrupting phrase or clause, so use *two commas* unless one is replaced by some other punctuation mark. It is easy to remember to use two commas if you compare them to parentheses.

You have a choice about punctuating explanatory information. If you believe the explanation limits or restricts or defines the modified word, it is functioning as a restrictive phrase that answers the question "which one?" and thus narrows the sentence to that subcategory. A restrictive phrase is *not* set off with commas.

> Tomorrow you can use the car that is in the garage. (*there are other cars around*)

On the other hand, if the explanatory information does not restrict the meaning but is instead merely useful, you can choose to relegate it to a subordinate position through the use of commas.

> Tomorrow you can drive my car, which is in the garage. (*only one car*)

A nonrestrictive phrase or clause describes, or gives additional information about, the *entire* category that has already been named.

> The cars, **which** are imported through the West coast, cost more than $45,000 each. (*All in this group of cars cost more than $45,000—their importation point is not essential to narrow the group.*)

> The cars **that** are imported through the West coast cost more than $45,000 each. (*Of many different cars, these cars (i.e., a limited group) that came from the West coast cost more.*)

(5) When you have written a sentence that cannot be read aloud in one breath but contains essential clauses you cannot delete, you have a fall-back option of throwing in a "breather" comma.

> In addition to its place in our legal heritage, English law is interesting today both for the comparative

dimension it adds to law study by showing how another member of the common law family of jurisdictions deals with current legal issues, and for the intrinsic interest of following legal developments in one of the leading western industrial democracies.

The sentence is balanced and well thought out, but too long for comfort. The comma adds the comfort factor.

(6) A set of commas allows legal writers to insert necessary citation into their texual discussion. Legal readers therefore have the option of reading each part of a citation carefully or slipping right over the entire citation; that option is signaled by a pair of commas. This practice of setting a citation apart from the text, but keeping it within the sentence itself, adds variety to the practice of placing the documentation after the end of each sentence. Remember, however, that citations within the text of legal sentences can create too much bulk if overused.

The 1975 court, in <u>Mokry v. University of Texas Health Science Center</u>, 529 S.W.2d 802 (Tex. Civ. App.—Dallas 1975, writ ref'd n.r.e.), also recognized a case within the Tort Claims Act when the hospital's failure to employ the equipment available led to the loss of the plaintiff's eyeball while it was being prepared for examination after surgical removal.

B. Use a semicolon.

Semicolons allow for a slightly longer pause when the sentence's commas are busy slowing readers down just a bit. The semicolon can help distinguish between short and slightly longer pauses that distinguish items in a list. Examine the following sentence, for instance, that uses only commas:

The plaintiff ate at Little Pizza Restaurants in Phoenix, Arizona, Lubbock, Texas, Boca Raton, Florida, and Bloomington, Illinois, before she learned that Little Pizza does not flash-freeze hamburger meat.

You could use a semicolon to signal a slightly longer pause between the major divisions:

REVISION

The plaintiff ate at Little Pizza Restaurants in Phoenix, Arizona; Lubbock, Texas; Boca Raton, Florida; and Bloomington, Illinois, before she learned that Little Pizza does not flash-freeze hamburger meat.

IV. To help readers SEPARATE ITEMS IN A SERIES:

A. Use commas between each item, including the last.

Although the comma before an "and" or "or" in a series is optional in other types of writing, legal writers' options are narrowed because of the need for precision. Look, for instance, at this correctly punctuated series:

He was charged with assault and battery, breaking and entering, and rape.

To drop the comma after "entering" would invite the readers' eyes to zoom through three charges, all introduced with "and" but not divided ("breaking and entering and rape"). The comma before the final "and" is essential to readers who cannot divide lists as they first process the sentence. In the next example, the first comma slows readers down and creates an expectation of a second—and third—clause. The two "and"s before "qualified" and "manage" make it difficult for readers to group and regroup without a complete rereading.

Williams is financially solvent, an experienced businessman and qualified to own and manage the shop.

Thus, legal writers punctuate before the final conjunction in a series.

B. *Use semicolons if you add a nonrestrictive modifier to any of the items in a list.*

The semicolon functions between listed items as a big comma. It asks for a pause similar to the pause signaled by commas for a modifier but nevertheless insists on a longer pause than one for mere parenthetical information.

Freshlaws study contracts, which emphasizes the power of the word, civil procedure, which reviews railroads and history, property, a course of heirs and next-of-kins, and torts, which offers recognizable fact situations.

REVISION

Freshlaws study contracts, which emphasizes the power of the word; civil procedure, which reviews railroads and history; property, a course of heirs and next-of-kins; and torts, which offers recognizable fact situations.

V. To OFFER A LIST:

When the list is a grammatical part of the sentence, the items to be enumerated must belong to the same class, with a common idea introduced before the colon. Then, for lists within a formal text, writers can choose to set the list apart from the text:

1. by introducing the list with a colon;
2. by indenting each item and numbering each item;
3. by beginning each item with a lowercase letter;
4. by concluding each item but the last with a semicolon;
5. by placing a semicolon and "and" or "or" after the next-to-last item; and
6. by concluding the item with a period unless the list does not conclude the textual sentence.

If writers choose to create a list that follows a complete sentence but is not a part of the textual sentence's grammar, then they must switch capitalization and punctuation conventions to match. Writers should follow the following seven conventions:

1. Colon introduction.
2. Indentation.
3. Grammatically parallel.
4. Capital letters.
5. Numbered items.
6. Periods at the end of each item.
7. No "or" or "and" for culmination.

If legal writers create an informal document or want to highlight a series of items that are not necessarily grammatically parallel, they can use bullet dots and other typographical cues instead of numbers.

VI. To PULL WORDS TOGETHER so readers recognize a thought unit:

Use a hyphen.

(1) When writers choose to combine two adjectives into one descriptive adjective before a noun, they combine the adjectives with a hyphen:

The state sponsored negotiators offered a week of free negotiations to help clear the courts' dockets.

This string of words before the noun functions as a compound adjective and needs to be hyphenated: *the state-sponsored nego-tiators.* The hyphen creates a bond between the two words so that they can correctly be read as a compound adjective before the main noun "negotiators." Remember, however, that adverbs ending in -*ly* cannot be hyphenated.

(2) If two nouns function as modifiers before a given noun, writers generally choose to hyphenate them to reflect their relationship (*see* Chapter 3):

the repair limitation provision
the repair-limitation provision

Once hyphenated, the noun-modifier units are broken from the string and help readers locate the noun. A second option to clarify these noun strings is to relocate portions of them away from the string:

the provision that limits repair

VII. To PUSH WORDS APART from the text so readers recognize the need for a long pause:

A. Use a dash.

Dashes signal a break in thought and writing—and thus legal writers are more reluctant to use them than, for instance, novelists are. But dashes have their place in any writing. Dashes can function like a colon, indicating something will follow an independent clause. Therefore, if the connection is obvious and you want to emphasize that a classifying clause follows, the dash remains a cautious option:

The court has one consistent goal—to provide justice for the people of this state.

Dashes differ from hyphens in both typography and purpose. On a typewriter or computer, writers type dashes with two hyphens and no spaces on either side. Dashes *separate*; hyphens draw together.

The red-hot issue this semester was faculty diversity.

Faculty diversity was an issue across the campus this semester--a hot issue.

B. Use a colon.

Colons signal that material promised or suggested will follow; thus, quotations, questions, explanations, and enumerations follow a colon.

Our law firm has only two rules: (1) research, research, research, and (2) the boss is always right.

The study involved the banking records of three states: Pennsylvania, New Jersey, and Oklahoma.

Colons are used to introduce material that is not a normal part of the sentence's grammar. Writers should not use them between a verb and its complement or object, between a preposition and its object, or after "such as" and "including" unless the material to follow is tabulated on separate lines.

On Thursday he wrote: three memoranda and two client letters.

REVISION

On Thursday he wrote three memoranda and two client letters.

The clerk had noticeable quirks such as: he refused to answer any question not written on a 3 X 5 card, he referred to attorneys as "Mr. Attorney" and "Miss Attorney," and he refused to work on Saturdays.

REVISION

The clerk had noticeable quirks: he refused to answer any question not written on a 3 X 5 card, he referred to attorneys as "Mr. Attorney" and "Miss Attorney," and he refused to work on Saturdays.

Capitalization after a colon is optional, but most writers capitalize complete sentences after the colon and leave fragments in lowercase:

We must all accept a priority: Your priority was never on my list.

The student went to law school for personal reasons: his bank account and his parents.

VIII. To signal a DIRECT QUOTATION or A WORD USED AS A WORD:

Use quotation marks.

Legal writers frequently have the option of either paraphrasing ideas or using direct quotations, but once the decision is made to quote someone's actual words, then quotation marks are required.

(1) You must use quotation marks when you quote a word or phrase within your text:

The attorney was worried about the "chilling effect of the undocumented evidence." [Cite.]

(2) In writing legal memoranda and briefs, if you have a quotation that is longer than 49 words (or if you have a special reason for setting quoted material outside your main text), signal the indented quotation with a single-spaced indented format but do *not* use quotation marks: The formatting signals the direct quotation. If the quotation is not a part of your textual sentence, lead into it with a colon. If the quotation picks up your textual syntax, do not add any punctuation before indenting and single spacing.

The number of judges cannot keep up with the demands of society. We need more judges:

> For example, in less than two decades, the total number of filings in California has increased 176% in the Supreme Court and 438% in the courts of appeal, yet there has been no like increase in the number of judges. . . . During this period, the number of Supreme Court justices remained the same. [During the same period,] the Arizona Supreme Court filings increased from 321 to 1,083 (238%); New Mexico, 194 to 1,254 (547%). In both Arizona and New Mexico, the number of appellate judges remained the same.

S. Eric Ottesen, Effective Brief-Writing for California Appellate Courts, 21 San Diego L. Rev. 371, 373 & nn. 9-10 (1980) (footnotes omitted).

The number of judges cannot keep up with the demands of society. According to S. Eric Ottesen, we need more judges because in less than twenty years

> the total number of filings in California has increased 176% in the Supreme Court and 438% in the courts of appeal, yet there has been no like increase in the number of judges. . . . During this period, the number of Supreme Court justices

> remained the same. [During the same period,] the
> Arizona Supreme Court filings increased from 321
> to 1,083 (238%); New Mexico, 194 to 1,254 (547%). In
> both Arizona and New Mexico, the number of
> appellate judges remained the same.

Effective Brief-Writing for California Appellate Courts,
21 San Diego L. Rev. 371, 373 & nn. 9-10 (1980)
(footnotes omitted).

(3) You can use quotation marks to highlight that a word
is intended to mean something different from its original
definition:

> His idea of a "great time" was to review last week's
> cases.

A second option is italics:

> His idea of a *great time* was to review last week's cases.

(4) Quotation marks enclose words you will define:

> By "successful student," the law school means some-
> one with grades good enough for law review.

Italics may be used here also:

> By *successful student*, the law school means someone
> with grades good enough for law review.

IX. To WARN readers that you have ALTERED QUOTED TEXT:

A. *Use ellipses.*

Ellipses indicate that you have chosen to omit material from a passage being quoted. (An ellipsis mark is composed of three spaced periods.) When you omit material after a period in the text, you add a fourth dot to include the final punctuation mark; the first dot is the period, so you type no space between it and the preceding word if the original text includes a period. If you omit material before that sentence ends, then follow it with a space before the first dot.[1] You should have a complete sentence on both sides of the four-dot ellipsis:

> In 1942 the Chief Justice of the United States, Mr. Justice Frankfurter, received a letter from a boy of twelve who announced his ambition to be a lawyer one day. . . . The Chief Justice wrote back encouragingly, telling the boy to forget about the law . . . and to concentrate on improving his mind and his appreciation of language by reading good literature, looking at good pictures and generally learning to be a cultured, civilized person. . . . "No one," he wrote, "can truly be a competent lawyer unless he is a cultivated man. The best way to prepare for the law is to come to the study of law as as well-read man. Thus alone can one acquire the capacity to use the English language on paper and in speech and with the habits of clear thinking which only a truly liberal education can give."[2]

Legal writers do not use ellipsis points before a block quotation beginning with a complete sentence even though they have (usually) left out material from the original.

---

1. THE BLUEBOOK: A UNIFORM SYSTEM OF CITATION Rule 5.1(a) (15th ed. 1991).

2. KENNETH HUDSON, THE JARGON OF THE PROFESSIONS 19 (1978), quoting from LOUIS BLOM-COOPER, THE LANGUAGE OF THE LAW 357 (1965).

B. Use brackets.

Legal writers must be scrupulous about indicating any changes they have made in quoting the words of another author.[3] For legal writers, brackets signal

1. missing words or letters;
2. capitals changed to lowercase and lowercase words changed to capitals to fit the sense of the quotation into your text;
3. additions that help explain ambiguous material in a quotation;
4. your own comments inserted into quoted material; and
5. the word "sic" to indicate an error repeated from the original ("sic" is a complete word meaning "in this manner" or "thus").

Following are examples of correctly placed brackets:

Nelson suggested, "Phillip Grandwell's statement [made directly after Sarah Grandwell threatened to take William to New Orleans] was part of a casual conversation and was never intended to be a serious comment."

The contract specifically provides that "$10,000 shall be paid to the surrogate [appellant] upon entry of the judgment fully terminating parental rights of the surrogate." <u>See</u> Surrogate Mother Contract Agreement § 4.

"[T]he intention of the Legislature, once ascertained, is the law." <u>Lone Star Gas Co. v. State</u>, 159 S.W.2d 681,

---

3. THE BLUEBOOK: A UNIFORM SYSTEM OF CITATION Rule 5.2 (15th ed. 1991).

692 (Tex. 1941). In ascertaining legislative intent, this court has made it clear that "[i]t is for the courts to ascertain—neither add nor subtract, neither delete nor distort [legislative intent]." <u>Commissioner v. Mercantile Nat'l Bank</u>, 276 F.2d 58, 62 (5th Cir. 1960).

According to Wilson's letter, Cunningham is "indecent [sic] until proven guilty."

Practice with Punctuation

Decide if the following sentences are properly punctuated to get across the message quickly and smoothly.

1. Mr. Brown requests damages, litigation costs and attorneys' fees.

2. The court held that, because Mr. Hall had alleged the time and place of the violation, the conduct that interfered with his rights, and the persons responsible for the violation, his complaint was sufficiently specific to provide the defendant with adequate notice.

3. However, to be granted judicial relief for misappropriation of a trade secret the plaintiff must prove by a preponderance of the evidence the following elements.

4. Courts are becoming increasingly more likely to determine that employer established welfare benefit plans are covered by ERISA.

5. The issue of the insolvency of a debtor is a question of fact and solvency may be determined proximately before or immediately after the time of the transfer.

6. However the decision in <u>Struthers Wells</u> was written prior to the adoption of paragraph (k).

7. The suit should have been brought against W. S. McBeath, Administrator of the Alcoholic Beverage Commission, Ann Richards, the State Treasurer, and Jim Mattox, the Attorney General.

8. Course and scope of employment is defined in section 101.001(B)(4) as:

> . . . the performance for a governmental unit of the duties of an employee's office of employment and includes being in or about the performance of tasks lawfully assigned to an employee by competent authority.

Possible Answers

1. *(Punctuation of legal **series** requires final comma:)* Mr. Brown requests damages, litigation costs, and attorneys' fees.

2. *(Comma asked to perform too many tasks; **rewrite** to allow commas to signal series only:)* The court held that Mr. Hall's complaint was sufficiently specific to provide the defendant with adequate notice because Mr. Hall had alleged the time and place of the violation, the conduct that interfered with his rights, and the persons responsible for the violation.

The court held Mr. Hall had alleged the time and place of the violation, the conduct that interfered with his rights, and the persons responsible for the violation; **thus**, his complaint was sufficiently specific to provide the defendant with adequate notice.

3. *(Comma needed after introductory infinitive phrase to separate it from the main subject:)* However, to be granted judicial relief for misappropriation of a trade secret, the plaintiff must prove by a preponderance of the evidence the following elements.

4. *(**Hyphens** needed for noun strings—unless they contradict existing statutes that consistently use them in*

unhyphenated form:) Courts are becoming increasingly more likely to determine that employer-established welfare-benefit plans are covered by ERISA.

5. *(Comma between **two independent clauses** is especially important when the object of the first verb and subject of the second sentence can be confused:)* The issue of the insolvency of a debtor is a question of fact, and solvency may be determined proximately before or immediately after the time of the transfer.

6. *(Comma after **introductory adverbial** to allow a pause for clarity:)* However, the decision in <u>Struthers Wells</u> was written prior to the adoption of paragraph (k).

7. *(Semicolons needed to **separate major and minor levels** within a list:)* The suit should have been brought against W. S. McBeath, Administrator of the Alcoholic Beverage Commission; Ann Richards, the State Treasurer; and Jim Mattox, the Attorney General.

8. *(Quotation marks needed around defined term; no colon after "as" within text; length of quotation does not require a single-spaced block, and no ellipses needed at the beginning of a quotation:)* "Course and scope of employment" is defined in section 101.001(B)(4) as "the performance for a governmental unit of the duties of an employee's office of employment and includes being in or about the performance of tasks lawfully assigned to an employee by competent authority."

Add punctuation that responds to the goal listed.

1. *(stop but go, or to signal a saying follows)* "There are obviously two educations. One should teach us how to make a living and the other how to live." THE INTERNATIONAL DICTIONARY OF THOUGHTS 240 (John P. Bradley et al. eds., 1969) (quoting James Truslow Adams).

2. *(separate a contradictory prepositional phrase from the rest of the sentence)* "The chief object of education is not to learn things but to unlearn things." G.K. Chesterton.

3. *(separate two sentences)* "My mother wanted me to have an education so she got me out of school." WIT AND WISDOM (Colin Bingham ed., 1982) (quoting Margaret Mead).

4. *(change nonrestrictive element to restrictive)* "The 'School of Hard Knocks' beloved of businessmen is a somewhat unstructured comprehensive." Lord Vaisey, 1983 *Observer.*

5. *(slow down reader)* "We don't have but greatly need a training culture." Norman Willis, *A Worker's Right to Train*, NATIONAL WESTMINISTER BANK QUARTERLY REVIEW, 1989.

6. *(speed up reader)* "If you think law is just something to enable you to get a Volvo, while you are waiting for your parents to die, and leave you with their superfluous wealth, then you really should be doing something else." Chris Murphy's address to law students reported in *Sydney Morning Herald.*

Possible Answers

1. *(colon or dash)* "There are obviously two educations: One should teach us how to make a living and the other how to live."

"There are obviously two educations—one should teach us how to make a living and the other how to live."

2. *(dash or comma)* "The chief object of education is not to learn things—but to unlearn things."

"The chief object of education is not to learn things, but to unlearn things."

3. *(period or comma with conjunction)* "My mother wanted me to have an education. So she got me out of school."

"My mother wanted me to have an education, so she got me out of school."

4. *(add two commas)* "The 'School of Hard Knocks,' beloved of businessmen, is a somewhat unstructured comprehensive."

5. *(add commas)* "We don't have, but greatly need, a training culture."

6. *(delete unnecessary commas)* "If you think law is just something to enable you to get a Volvo while you are waiting for your parents to die and leave you with their superfluous wealth, then you really should be doing something else."

Justify the use of either a colon or a semicolon in these sentences.

1. Each of the Constitution's Amendments has the same purpose each protects us from ourselves.

2. Not many freshmen are self-confident certainly we can list those in our section.

Possible Answers

1. After a colon, the second clause would state the purpose. After a semicolon, the clause would continue the idea.

2. A semicolon would continue the idea. A colon would work only if the second clause had been more closely related; e.g., *Not many of our freshmen are self-confident: self-aware, yes.*

ADDITIONAL EXERCISES
(See Possible Answers in Appendix at page 190.)

Practice with Punctuation

Read the following sentences and decide if they are properly punctuated to get the message across quickly. Some of the sentences may be incorrect; most sentences contain a punctuation option that provides either clearer meaning or smoother reading.

1. Mr. Brown also claims that during the arrest Officer Smith became "highly abusive", denied Mr. Brown his right to speak and struck the plaintiff twice, without provocation, causing him bodily injury.

2. In the decision in <u>Santex,</u> supra, the court also held that the employee need prove only that filing the claim was a reason for termination not the sole reason.

3. Plaintiff further argued that the statute did not apply because the unit was only a component part of a larger whole; thus not, by itself, an "improvement."

4. The Texas Supreme Court has stated that, generally, common law indemnity is grounded in either (1) different qualities of negligence; (2) a breach of duty between tortfeasors; or (3) vicarious liability. <u>Bonniwell v. Beech Aircraft Corp.,</u> 663 S.W.2d 816, 823 (Tex. 1984).

5. The common law doctrine of negligence consists of three essential elements—a legal duty owed by one person to another, a breach of that duty and damages proximately caused by that breach. <u>See</u> <u>Rosas v. Buddy's Food Store,</u> 518 S.W.2d 534, 536 (Tex. 1975).

6. The second issue of first impression is whether the reservation of the power to prosecute, compromise and settle or otherwise deal with any claim for additional royalties is illegal

and void as an attempt to engage in the unauthorized practice of law.

7. A statement apparently made to the EEOC by Weeks shows that Weeks spends only 50% of his time developing new business; whereas, Johnson spent all of his time developing new business. (Document Response No. 6). Weeks also states that when he began his employment at the Bank, he assumed 1/3 of Johnson's loans; while Bowers and Ehrenpreis evenly split the remaining loans.

8. The decisions holding that a creditor of the promise can maintain action on the contract of which he is the beneficiary have been based upon no one well-defined theory.

9. Likewise, Oxy's and Mobil's attempt to invoke the inherent jurisdiction of the District Court pursuant to Article 5, section 8 of the Texas Constitution, sections 24.007, 24.008 and 24.011 of the Texas Government Code, and section 85.241 of the Texas Natural Resources Code, is not proper.

10. Such participation, he claims was fundamentally unfair.

11. The Comptroller's audit assessment was correct, because the seven (7) customer contracts stated material and equipment, labor and sales tax as separated amounts; making these seven (7) contracts separated contracts under Section 151.056.

12. Defendants committed to provide 370 psychiatric acute care beds in facilities that conform to the new standards.

13. In addition, this group was charged with developing proposals by which the state funded health education institutions could assist or augment TDC.

Compare the following versions of the same sentence. (1) Which is the most matter-of-fact? (2) Which allows a longer pause and perhaps greater emphasis on "his best friend"? (3) Which creates the longest pause? (4) Which has a formal, almost solemn quality?

A. He did not intend to defraud Mr. Adams, his best friend.

B. He did not intend to defraud Mr. Adam—his best friend.

C. He did not intend to defraud Mr. Adams: his best friend.

APPENDIX I

Grammar and Punctuation Reviews

GRAMMAR CHECK # 1

Edit any grammar errors in the following sentences. (Some sentences may be correct; others may be stylistically awkward but grammatically correct.)

1. Registration exhausted Wendy, so she decided to lay down for an hour.

2. Pulling down her window shades, her comfort and privacy were assured.

3. She chose not to answer whomever was calling her.

4. Instead, she decided to pull the pillow over her head and sticking her fingers in her ears.

5. Neither the casebooks nor the first professor would be as intimidating as her classmates.

6. Wendy Jones sleeping through the first day of classes was considered unusual.

7. However, the administration had plenty of experience with this before.

GRAMMAR CHECK # 2

1. Mary would never have known about or checked into the will that her cousin Fred found left to her own devices.

2. The uncle had told Mary that she would receive the largest portion of his estate to be divided between her and Fred.

3. There was barely no time at all to protest the newly found will.

4. The uncle's maid called Mary to say she had past the desk every day but had never seen a will on it.

5. Naturally, each of the heirs had their version of the uncle's promises.

6. Mary and Fred's versions differed the most.

7. Hearing about their protests, Mary and Jerry were called into the office of the uncle's attorney.

Answers to Grammar Reviews

Note: Corrections can vary.

Grammar Check #1

1. (*word choice*) Registration exhausted Wendy, so she decided to **lie** down for an hour.

2. (*dangling element*) Pulling down her window shades, **Wendy ensured** her comfort and privacy.

3. (*pronoun case: objective vs. nominative*) She chose not to answer **whoever** was calling her.

4. (*parallelism*) Instead, she decided **to pull** the pillow over her head and **stick** her fingers in her ears.

5. (*correct as is*) Neither the casebooks nor the first professor would be as intimidating as her classmates.

6. (*gerund requires possessive*) Wendy **Jones'** sleeping through the first day of classes was considered unusual.

7. (*ambiguous pronoun*) However, the administration had plenty of experience with **this syndrome** before.

Grammar Check # 2

1. (*misplaced modifier*) Mary, **left to her own devices,** would never have known about or checked into the will that her cousin Fred found.

2. (*comparative vs. superlative*) The uncle had told Mary that she would receive the **larger** portion of his estate to be divided between her and Fred.

3. (*excessive negatives*) There was **barely time** at all to protest the newly found will.

4. (*word choice*) The uncle's maid called Mary to say she had **passed** the desk every day but had never seen a will on it.

5a. (*pronoun/antecedent*) Naturally, each of the heirs had **his or her own** version of the uncle's promises.

b. Both heirs had **their** versions of the uncle's promises.

6. (*possessive*) **Mary's** and Fred's versions differed the most.

7. (*dangling element*) Hearing about their protests, **the uncle's attorney** called Mary and Fred into his office.

PUNCTUATION CHECK # 1

Correct any punctuation error in the following formal report.

1. The policeman, responding to the caller asked, "Are you having a problem here"?

2. The clerk nodded her head up and down but she did not utter a word.

3. Concerned, the policeman looked up and down the aisles of merchandise, and checked into each rest room.

4. When he had satisfied himself that the store was empty except for the clerk the policeman returned to the cashier's desk.

5. Now the clerk talked excitedly about the stolen items, such as a cooler, Styrofoam, that the thief had used as a basket, a transistor radio, the new sporty version with a wrist strap, and two six packs of beer.

6. As he wrote, dividing the items into approximate value rows of numbers he patiently asked leading questions designed to help the clerk recall details.

7. The owners new security system had not worked because the clerk did not have the early detection code.

PUNCTUATION CHECK # 2

1. The horse sale was completed, all that was needed was the contract.

2. The owners wanted the horse which was gray to have its brand changed immediately.

3. The horse swatting his tail suddenly concerned the new owner who worried about twitching diseases.

4. Any owner, worrying about details, can forget, or at least seem to, the larger picture, because what is wrong seems so ominous that the good points recede. Like a contract clause covering diseases.

5. The following were listed under "Diseases:" . . .

6. The owner could have waited to read the contract however he called his groom, canceled the sale and left town to find a different horse to buy.

Answers to Punctuation Reviews

Punctuation Check #1

1. *(Question mark location depends on what part of the sentence is a question. Here, the quotation contains the question and the mark thus belongs inside the quotation marks. No additional terminal punctuation is needed; the period at the bottom of the question mark serves as a period for the entire sentence.)* The policeman, responding to the caller asked, "Are you having a problem **here?"**

2. *(comma necessary between two independent clauses separated by a conjunction)* The clerk nodded her head up and **down, but** she did not utter a word.

3. *(comma incorrectly separates second verb from its subject)* Concerned, the policeman **looked up** and down the aisles of merchandise **and checked** into each rest room.

4. *(comma necessary after introductory adverbial clause)* When he had satisfied himself that the store was empty except for the **clerk,** the policeman returned to the cashier's desk.

5. *(no comma necessary before "such as"; semicolons necessary in list that contains commas used for parenthetical modifiers)* Now the clerk talked excitedly about the stolen **items such as** a cooler, Styrofoam, that the thief had used as a **basket;** a transistor radio, the new sporty version with a wrist **strap;** and two six packs of beer.

6. *(two commas needed to delineate parenthetical modifier)* As he wrote, dividing the items into approximate value

rows of **numbers,** he patiently asked leading questions designed to help the clerk recall details.

7. (*possessive*) The **owner's** new security system had not worked because the clerk did not have the early detection code.

Punctuation Check # 2

1. *(comma splice; comma alone cannot separate two independent clauses)* The horse sale was **completed. All** that was needed was the contract.

2. *(nonessential modifiers need commas to set them off; correct without commas if the description is essential)* The owners wanted the **horse, which was gray,** to have its brand changed immediately.

3. *(punctuation of possessive before a gerund; **optional** comma to separate relative pronoun clause)* The **horse's** swatting his tail suddenly concerned the new **owner,** who worried about twitching diseases.

4. *(Excessive commas create choppy reading; option to drop some or reword. Incorrect comma separates verb from following adverbial clause. Period creates fragment.)* Any owner worrying about details can forget, or at least seem to, the larger **picture because** what is wrong seems so ominous that the good points recede—like a contract clause covering diseases.

5. *(quotation marks require commas and periods inside, colons and semicolons outside)* The following were listed under "Diseases": . . .

6. *(Run-on requires terminal punctuation. Series requires comma before "and" or "or.")* The owner could have waited to read the **contract. However**, he called his groom, canceled the **sale, and** left town to find a different horse to buy.

APPENDIX II

Annotated Student Examples

I. Student Memorandum

This memorandum deals with only one issue; a judge has asked his clerk for a tentative answer. The student states the law as it applies to one assigned case. Notice the quick pace of the memorandum: It focuses only on the question and the balance of cases that pertain to the issue. You should find a balanced, objective content paralleled by a clear and concise tone.*

---

*Memo edited by Fred Asnes.

FACTS PRESENTED

Harry Evans is a member of the United Mine Workers and a recruiter for its Local 101. He competes in recruiting members with Progressive Miners of America. The competition is stiff. On one occasion at a membership drive, an altercation occurred during which Evans' left arm was shot off by James Keck, a recruiter for the Progressive Miners of America. Evans has brought suit in federal district court in Illinois against Keck, a citizen of Illinois, and against the Progressive Miners of America, an unincorporated association with its headquarters in West Virginia but with no members or activities outside West Virginia and Illinois. Evans claims $500,000 in damages.

At the time Evans' arm was shot off, he resided in Illinois, being employed as a miner there. He had lived in Illinois his entire life, as had his father before him. After his injury, but before filing suit, he moved to Oklahoma, where he took up farming. He is licensed to drive and is registered to vote in Oklahoma, where he claims he intends to reside.

Defendants have moved under Federal Rule of Civil Procedure 12(b)(1) to dismiss for lack of subject matter jurisdiction, alleging that Evans is a citizen of Illinois. They offer the following proof: 1) the funds for Evans' move to Oklahoma, as well as the funds establishing Evans' farming operation, were provided by the United Mine Workers; 2) Evans is still a member of the United Mine Workers, though it has no activities in Oklahoma; and 3) Evans told Harry Morgan, a fellow miner, that as soon as the case against Keck and the Progressive Miners of America was settled, Evans would consider moving back to Illinois.

Does this federal court have jurisdiction?

M E M O R A N D U M

September 20, 1984

TO: Judge

FROM: Student

SUBJECT: Evans v. Keck and
          Progressive Miners of
          America

Question Presented

Does the federal court have
jurisdiction in this case?

Discussion

Plaintiff Evans alleges that the
Court has jurisdiction over this
case pursuant to 28 U.S.C.
§ 1332(a)(1) (1982). Jurisdiction
under this section has two
requisites. First, the matter in
controversy must exceed the sum or
value of $10,000, exclusive of
interests and costs. There is no
dispute that this case satisfies
this jurisdictional amount;
plaintiff lost his arm and seeks
$500,000.00. See Cunningham v.

****

Readers' responses to substantive information appear in margin.

****

[Readers' concerns about grammar, punctuation, and style appear in brackets.]

****

be more specific

statement of
case, but where
is conclusion?

["alleges" sets
proper tentative
tone]

set-up of two
requisites is
strong organiza-
tional tool, esp.
with "first"
follow-up

distinguishes what is *not* the pertinent question

Ford Motor Co., 413 F. Supp. 1101 (D.S.C. 1976).

---

new topic sentence highlights second prong

pertinent language quoted directly

contrary position of plaintiff

[repetition of "undisputed" and "not questioned" effectively sets aside disputed points]

[what does "takes the citizenship" mean?]

Second, complete diversity of citizenship must exist between the parties. Strawbridge v. Curtiss, 7 U.S. 267 (1806). It is "citizenship at the time of filing suit" that is controlling. Gordon v. Steele, 376 F. Supp. 575 (W.D. Pa. 1974). Plaintiff Evans alleges that he is a citizen of Oklahoma. Defendants have moved under Federal Rule of Civil Procedure 12(b)(1) to dismiss for lack of subject matter jurisdiction, alleging that Evans is a citizen of Illinois. It is undisputed that Keck is a citizen of Illinois. It is also not questioned that the Progressive Miners of America (PMA), as an unincorporated association, takes the citizenship of all its members: West Virginia and Illinois. See Navarro Sav. Assn. v. Lee, 446 U.S. 458 (1980).

concise topic sentence

rule and its language, court interpretation, and citation followed by application to present case

Plaintiff has the burden of establishing his citizenship. Gordon, 376 F. Supp. at 576. To be a citizen within the meaning of § 1332(a)(1), a natural person must be a citizen of the United States and a domiciliary of the state in which he claims citizenship. Mas v. Perry, 489 F.2d 1396 (5th Cir. 1979). A domiciliary

is one who resides in the state and
intends to reside there indefinitely. Gordon, 376 F. Supp. at 577.
Evans offers the following evidence
to establish his claim of domicile.
At the time of filing suit, he was   balanced
residing and farming in Oklahoma. He   presentation of
is licensed to drive and registered   both sides
to vote in Oklahoma. On the question
of intent, Evans claims he intends
to continue his residency there.

   Defendants offer the following   strong summary
controverting evidence. The funds   topic sentence
for Evans' move to Oklahoma, as well
as the funds establishing Evans'
farming operation, were provided by
the United Mine Workers. Also, Evans   [effective
is still a member of the United Mine   transitions: *also,*
Workers, though it has no activities   *finally, from*
in Oklahoma. Finally, the most   *these facts*]
damaging evidence. Evans told Harry
Morgan, a fellow miner, that as soon
as the case against Keck and the PMA
was settled, Evans would consider
moving back to Illinois. From these
facts, defendants argue that while   smooth shift
Evans obviously resides in Oklahoma,   from facts to
he is not a domiciliary of Oklahoma   argument
since he went to Oklahoma for the
sole purpose of attempting to
manipulate diversity jurisdiction
and without a sincere intention to
reside there indefinitely.

   While changing residence to
create diversity jurisdiction is not
necessarily inconsistent with an
intention to remain in one's new

147

court language
paraphrased,
with citation

application of
definition to
facts of case

residence indefinitely, one's motive in moving may be evidence of one's intent. Thus, the question is intention at the time of arrival in the new residence. Id. at 578. If Evans intended to reside there indefinitely, whatever the reason for his move, he made Oklahoma his domicile.

conclusion
paragraph

reason for
writer's opinion:
court efficiency

effective
integration of
quotation to
back up court
precedent for
dismissing or
overruling plain-
tiff's evidence

Even though Evans as a native of Illinois does not need the protection that diversity jurisdiction is designed to afford non-residents, and indeed may have moved to Oklahoma merely to achieve some tactical advantage in diversity jurisdiction, it is more efficient for this court to apply the bright-line rule of domicile than to sort out who does and who does not need the protection of diversity jurisdiction. Whatever Evans' motive for moving, given his attachment to his new community in this case, the court should be unwilling to find that Evans' own claim of intent is false. As for the statement to Harry Morgan, a fellow miner, "[i]t is not important if there is within contemplation a vague possibility of eventually going elsewhere, or even of returning whence one came." Id.

Thus, merely because Evans would consider moving back to Illinois does not belie his claimed intention to make Oklahoma his residence indefinitely. After all, indefinitely does not mean permanently.

[parallel structure within contrasting language ("in-definitely"/ "per-manently") is effective]

Defendants' motion to dismiss should be denied.

legal question more specific here; should be rephrased in introduction also.
Summarize *why* it should be denied.

II. Student Brief

Michael Shelby and Lisa Pennington's brief received Best Nationwide status in the American Trial Lawyers Association (ATLA) Mock Trial Regionals. Notice the external and internal cues of organization. Even the Table of Contents sets the order in which the authors want readers to learn about the case: They define, and later dismiss, the plaintiff's contention and then present their own theory. Investigate the incorporation of quoted material and paraphrase, achieved by the authors' use of smooth transitions. Finally, evaluate the "facts": Are they persuasive or too slanted?* All references to the record have been omitted.

The few original errors have been retained so readers can see that even award-winning writers can improve. The marginalia identify the more important problems. As in the Memorandum, annotations include (1) responses to substantive information and (2) concerns about grammar, punctuation, and style. The latter appear in brackets.

---

*Editorial annotations by Fred Asnes.

No. 84-5678

IN THE
STATE SUPERIOR COURT
WISHBONE COUNTY, WISHBONE

Katie Brennan,   *
                                  *
            Plaintiff,   *
                                  *
    v.   *
                                        CIVIL ACTION
                                        NO. 84-5678

Bobby Brown,   *
                                  *
                                  *
            Defendant.   *

DEFENDANT'S TRIAL BRIEF

The University of Texas   MICHAEL TAYLOR SHELBY
    School of Law   LISA HOWARD PENNINGTON

February 6, 1984   Counsel for Defendants

151

II. *Student Brief*

TABLE OF CONTENTS

Page

STATEMENT OF THE CASE

Pursuant to Wishbone Rev. Stat., Chap. P, § 1258 (1984), plaintiff Katie Brennan filed this wrongful death action against defendant, Bobby Brown, to recover damages for injuries suffered as a result of her husband's accidental death on July 10, 1982. Plaintiff alleges that Brown was negligent in placing himself in a position inviting rescue, that her husband met his death while acting as his voluntary rescuer, and that defendant had a duty to warn plaintiff's decedent of any potential danger that he might encounter.

> explains why the court is to hear the case— immediate information

Defendant contends that (1) because the decedent was acting in the capacity of a fireman, the plaintiff is precluded from recovering under the "Professional Rescuers" exception to the Rescue Doctrine, and (2) defendant owed decedent no duty to warn decedent because the defendant had no opportunity to warn and the danger was open and obvious. Furthermore, defendant urges that such omissions were not the proximate cause of decedent's injuries. Defendant contends that decedent's own contributory negligence (rash and imprudent conduct) was the singular proximate cause of his death.

> separate paragraph for defendant's response
>
> use of numbering helps readers anticipate later argument
>
> introduces both defense and offense

1

Statement of Facts leaves readers convinced that Brennan is foolhardy and unsuccessful at his job. Question of defendant's negligence is overshadowed by decedent's own negligence.

effective chronological presentation

deliberate word choice characterizes Brown as established, prepared, careful. [Is this too slanted?]

[note active verbs]

[parallel verbs "fracturing" and "suffering" elevate "abrasions"]

STATEMENT OF FACTS

The defendant, Bobby Brown, is an experienced hiker and outdoorsman and a lifetime resident of Wishbone County, Wishbone. In pursuit of his hobbies, Brown diligently studies mountaineering techniques and purchased specialized rock climbing boots. Having thus prepared himself for an afternoon of rock climbing, Brown returned on July 10, 1982, to an area that had long been familiar to him and carefully selected a small, 25-foot cliff located next to Wishbone County's mountain road.

After having successfully completed two-thirds of his ascent, Brown lost his footing and fell to the ground, fracturing his right leg and suffering multiple abrasions and contusions. Because of the severe injuries to his leg, Brown was unable to move from the base of the cliff. At approximately 8:45 p.m., the Wishbone County Fire Depart-

2

154

ment's dispatcher ordered the County's team of firemen, Joe Brennan and Tim Wilson, to "look for the accident" that had occurred near the mountain road. After arriving at the scene, the two men, trained in emergency medical techniques, radioed the search and rescue squad and then left their rescue truck to look for the accident victim. When they began to call out, Bobby Brown answered that he was "over here." The two men turned the headlights of their rescue truck toward the direction of Brown's voice and equipped themselves with portable medical kits and flashlights.

["ordered" sets up "duty" of Brown]

["trained" establishes professionalism]

In his haste to "look for the accident," Joe Brennan began to run and soon began slipping and sliding over the extremely irregular terrain. Brennan's fellow fireman, Tim Wilson, estimated that Brennan ran out approximately 150 feet in front of him. Brennan then warned his fellow rescuer, who was proceeding much more cautiously, to "watch out and try not to run on the rocks" because "it's too hard." Although it was dark, the truck's headlights and the portable flashlights provided the two men with enough visibility to see at least 150 feet, as Wilson could clearly make out Brennan in front of him.

slanted language paints Brennan as hasty and not cautious

chronological details

While his rescuers approached, Brown lay at the base of the escarpment, hysterical and disoriented by the pain of his

[word choice too slanted here]

3

II. Student Brief

[stilted language: "condition afforded him no opportunity"]

["articulated appreciation"?]

carefully sets up contrast between Brennan (unsuccessful) and other rescue squad (successful); shifts emphasis from Brennan's death to his lack of success in mission of duty

injuries. His condition afforded him no opportunity to warn the decedent of any potential hazards he might encounter. Despite Brennan's articulated appreciation of the dangerous mountain terrain, he ran off the edge of the cliff and fell to his death. Shortly thereafter, another rescue squad arrived at the scene and successfully evacuated both Brown and decedent.

ARGUMENT AND AUTHORITIES

I. OVERVIEW: PLAINTIFF'S THEORY OF RECOVERY

clear set-up

[note use of generic "plaintiff" vs. use of defendant's actual and therefore humanizing name]

Plaintiff asserts two principal theories of recovery against defendant. First, plaintiff alleges that Bobby Brown negligently endangered himself and others by undertaking an ascent of a hazardous cliff despite his apparent lack of expertise to do so. As a result of this negligence, plaintiff contends, defendant created a dangerous situation which invited the decedent's

4

unsuccessful attempt at rescue.
Accordingly, plaintiff urges that
she should be allowed recovery under
Wishbone's "Rescue Doctrine."

Alternatively, plaintiff asserts
that defendant owed and violated a
duty to warn the decedent of the
dangerous conditions present at the
scene of the original accident.
Specifically, plaintiff contends
that defendant's failure to warn
Brennan of the hazard posed by the
cliff was the direct and proximate
cause of the decedent's death.

transition
signals second
alternative

[word choice:
"asserts" and
"contends" allow
no suggestion of
fact]

Because each of these contentions
is legally spurious and directly
contravened by the great weight of
evidence in this case, defendant
urges this court to reject their
application as a means of recovery.
Additionally, defendant contends
that the only producing cause of
plaintiff's injuries resulted from
the contributory negligence of the
decedent. Accordingly, plaintiff
should be precluded from asserting
liability against defendant.

short conclusion
to the two
theories

[miscuing
"additionally"]

II. THE "RESCUE DOCTRINE" THEORY

A. The Doctrine

As noted, plaintiff's initial
theory of recovery is premised upon
application of the so-called "Rescue
Doctrine" to the facts of the
present case. That doctrine (which
has been recognized and followed by

all headings and
subheadings
would be more
effective if they
were complete
sentences or
even clauses

5

the Wishbone judiciary) can be summarized as follows:

> [W]here the defendant has negligently created a situation of peril for another, the defendant will be held in law to have caused the peril not only to the victim but also to his rescuer, and so to have caused any injury suffered by the rescuer in his rescue attempt. John Tiley, The Rescue Principle, 30 Mod. L. Rev. 25 (1974). See "Rescue Doctrine," 57 Am. Jur. 2d Negligence § 227 (1971), and cases cited therein.

Though the doctrine is on its face quite broad, the judiciary of the several states have developed stringent criteria for its application that act to significantly limit its scope. Restatement (Second) of Torts § 445(d) (1965). For example, the doctrine requires "a voluntary act by a rescuer who is prompted by a spontaneous, humane motive to save human life without any duty by virtue of his employment." Gillespie v. Washington, 395 A.2d 18, 20 (D.C. 1978); see also Krauth v. Geller, 157 A.2d 129, 131 (N.J. 1960). Additionally, the "rescuer" is obligated to conduct himself in a manner which is neither "rash nor imprudent," Kennedy v. Delaware Leasing Co., 441 F.2d 562, 564 (6th Cir. 1971); that is, he must behave in a fashion which is reasonable in light of the particular emergency confronting him. Id.; Altamuro v.

6

<u>Milner Hotel, Inc.</u>, 540 F. Supp. 870, 876 (E.D. Pa. 1982).

In order, then, to invoke the "Rescue Doctrine" as a means of recovery against the defendant, the plaintiff must successfully demonstrate three elements: (1) that the defendant negligently created a situation of peril for the decedent; (2) that the decedent owed no duty to attempt to aid the defendant by virtue of his position as a fireman/emergency medical technician, but merely did so out of a "spontaneous" motive to save life; and finally (3) that the decedent acted in a manner that was neither "rash nor imprudent." <u>See generally</u> Joel E. Smith, Annotation, <u>Liability of One Negligently Causing Fire for Injuries Sustained by Persons Other Than Firefighter in Attempt to Control Fire or to Save Life or Property</u>, 91 A.L.R.3d 1202 (1979) and cases cited therein. The evidence in this case fails to support any of these contentions.

B. Defendant Did Not Act Neg-
    ligently in Attempting to
    Scale the Rock Face

As indicated, in order for plaintiff to establish a cause of action under the Rescue Doctrine, there must be a threshold demonstration that some negligent act on the part of the defendant served to place both the defendant

Annotations (right margin):

here transition signals causal relationship—a strategic choice

tabulation indicates organization to follow

paragraph serves as conclusion and introduction to next section: Statement of Facts has already anticipated and emphasized plaintiff's defects in all three areas—a major organizational strategy

combines law and fact

7

159

incorporates word quote into paraphrase

and the decedent in "peril." 57 Am. Jur. 2d <u>Negligence</u> § 227 (1971). Accordingly, plaintiff must prove that defendant was somehow negligent in attempting to ascend the 25-foot rock face.

[sentence variety with short topic sentence creates emphasis]

[word choice slant: language contrasts a detailed picture against plaintiff's claims and leads to a logical conclusion]

No such proof is possible in this case. The evidence to be adduced at trial demonstrates clearly that defendant is a mature, 30-year-old accountant who was quite familiar with the area he was attempting to explore. He was an extremely experienced hiker and had walked the area immediately surrounding the rock face on many occasions prior to the accident. He had outfitted himself with the proper footwear for a climb of this type and had gone so far as to read a text on the subject of rock climbing prior to his attempt. Knowing that this was his first climb, he purposely chose a familiar rock face of modest size. Plaintiff's assertion of negligence on the part of defendant is therefore untenable.

C. Even If Defendant Is Found to Be Negligent, Plaintiff Is Barred from Recovery Because the Decedent Was Acting as a "Professional Rescuer" at the Time of the Accident

Should this Honorable Court disregard the substantial body of evidence outlined above and thereby

8

find sufficient plaintiff's allegations regarding defendant's negligence, a second and independent ground exists for denying plaintiff recovery under the Rescue Doctrine.

transitional introduction from "evidence" above to second theory

1. The Professional Rescue Doctrine

As noted, in order to establish a right of recovery under the simple "rescue" principle, plaintiff must demonstrate that the decedent's actions in attempting to rescue the defendant were prompted "by a spontaneous, humane motive to save human life, and which 'rescue' the rescuer had no duty to attempt in the sense of a legal obligation or in the sense of a duty fastened on him by virtue of his employment." Gillespie, 395 A.2d at 20; Krauth, 157 A.2d at 131; Nastasio v. Cinnamon, 295 S.W.2d 117, 120 (Mo. 1956).

again, complete sentence would be a more effective heading

smooth movement from statement of law into application of law

The rationale for this common law requirement of selflessness lies in the policy considerations underlying the Rescue Doctrine. Simply stated, society wishes to encourage otherwise disinterested individuals to act as "good Samaritans" in emergency situations whenever possible. Holden v. Chunestudey, 161 Cal. Rptr. 925 (Cal. Ct. App. 1980). The Rescue Doctrine serves as both sword and shield for these individuals, providing them with a means of recovering for any injuries

clear topic sentence

[effective use of "word quote" in paraphrase rather than longer direct quotation]

9

[paraphrase
easy to follow]

they may suffer, while simultaneously protecting them from legal
impediments to recovery such as contributory negligence or assumption
of risk. Tiley, <u>supra</u>, 30 Mod. L.
Rev. at 25, and cases cited therein.

effective topic
sentence

[difficult to un-
derstand verbs
separated like
this from their
nouns; break
into separate
sentences or
rewrite sentence
so that the
passive verb
"have been
held" is closer to
each subject]

definition
obviously
eliminates
Brown

emphasis on
law

[unobtrusive
placement of
citations here]

The same considerations dictate a
contrary rule for those who volun-
tarily place themselves in the role
of a "professional rescuer." Firemen
(both professional and voluntary),
<u>Buchanan v. Prickett & Sons</u>, 279
N.W.2d 855 (Neb. 1979), policemen,
<u>Mouncey v. Ellard</u>, 297 N.E.2d 43
(Mass. 1973), security guards,
<u>Krueger v. City of Anaheim</u>, 181 Cal.
Rptr. 631 (Cal. Ct. App. 1982), and
even doctors, <u>Carter v. Taylor
Diving & Salvage Co.</u>, 341 F. Supp.
628, 631 (E.D. La. 1972), <u>aff'd,</u> 470
F.2d 995 (5th Cir. 1973), have all
been held subject to the singular
exception to the Rescue Doctrine.
This exception has been termed the
"Professional Rescuer Doctrine." The
doctrine generally excludes from
coverage under the general Rescue
Doctrine those whose business it is
to save lives and prevent injury to
persons and property. It states that
those engaged in rescue work as part
of their employment may not, as a
matter of law, recover for injuries
sustained by them on the job, from
those whose negligence was the
proximate cause of the injuries.
<u>Maltman v. Sauer</u>, 530 P.2d 254
(Wash. 1975); <u>Spencer v. B.P. John
Furniture Corp.</u>, 467 P.2d 429 (Or.
1970).

10

2. Decedent Was Acting as a
   "Professional Rescuer" When He
   Attempted to Aid Defendant

It is indisputable that decedent
was employed as a professional
fireman/emergency medical technician
("EMT") by the County of Wishbone at
the time of his death. The critical
issue in this trial is whether the
decedent was acting within the scope
of his duties as a professional
fireman/EMT when he attempted his
ill-fated rescue of defendant.

strong topic
sentence

paragraph sets
up issue

focuses
attention on
issue

As has been demonstrated, firemen
fall squarely within the
"professional rescuer" exception to
the general Rescue Doctrine. In
fact, the Professional Rescuer
Doctrine is popularly referred to in
many jurisdictions as the "Firemen's
Rule." See generally 91 A.L.R.3d
1202, and cases cited therein.
Accordingly, a fireman who is
injured while carrying out his professional duties may not seek to
impose liability on those whose
negligence causes that injury.
Fowler V. Harper & Fleming James,
Jr., 2 The Law of Torts § 18.2
(1956).

has it been dem-
onstrated or is
this manipulation
too obvious?

moves from
conclusion to
support

[effective variety
of transitions]

One of the primary functions of
any fire department is to provide
and engage in rescue operations for
members of the community it serves.
Consequently, numerous jurisdictions
have recognized that "rescue work is
one of the principal duties of a

quick, terse
language for
definition

11

authority backs up definition	fireman." <u>Buchanan</u>, 279 N.W.2d at 860, and cases cited therein. As the attorney general of California has concluded, "Emergency medical and rescue services are essentially a component of fire protection services . . . rescue services are a necessary incident of fire protection." 64 Op. Cal. Att'y Gen. 558 (1981).
transition restates thesis	Despite this somewhat obvious recognition, many individuals employed as firemen have attempted to circumvent the restrictions of the Professional Rescuer Doctrine by asserting (much like plaintiff) that the injuries they have sustained were incurred not as a result of the execution of the "official" duties, but rather a result of an indivi-dual--and thus independent--act of heroism in an attempt to rescue a potential victim. With virtual
[strong verbs and slanted nouns: "rejected," "contentions"]	unanimity, the courts have rejected these contentions. 91 A.L.R.3d at 1209. The principal reason for such overwhelming disapproval of this theory of recovery was well stated by the Nebraska Supreme Court, when it reasoned, "It is not possible to draw a substantive distinction founded upon the particular task being performed. . . . Attempting to
longer section of quotation avoided through ellipses	distinguish between `fire fighting' and `rescue' operations is unacceptable. . . ." <u>Buchanan</u>, 279 N.W.2d at 860.

12

Defendant urges that this Honorable Court abstain from attempting such a gossamer distinction in the present case. The facts to be proven at trial will preclude plaintiff's recovery under the general Rescue Doctrine by placing the decedent squarely within the "Professional Rescuer" exception.

["gossamer": poetic word conjures up image of hazy and threadbare and also contrasts with "facts to be proven"]

D. Decedent's Conduct During the Course of the Emergency Was Both "Rash" and "Imprudent," Thus Independently Barring Recovery Under the "Rescue Doctrine"

[quotation marks emphasize essential concepts]

As will be discussed <u>infra</u>, <u>see</u> IV, decedent's conduct during the course of the rescue attempt can in no way be considered reasonable under the circumstances of this particular emergency. As noted, the Rescue Doctrine requires that the rescuer act in a manner that is neither "rash nor imprudent". Though defendant concedes that the standard of reasonableness is somewhat less in emergency situations, the rescuer is nevertheless under a duty to avoid reckless behavior. As will be discussed, the facts of this case demonstrate a complete lack of caution on the part of the decedent Thus, the Rescue Doctrine should not provide plaintiff with a mechanism for recovery.

[first phrase is dead weight here; move to end of sentence]

[incorrect punctuation; belongs inside quotation marks]

["though defendant concedes" suggests writer is trying to be fair]

13

again, headings
should help
argue

III. "DUTY TO WARN" THEORY

Plaintiff's second means of recovery is premised upon the misguided assumption that defendant was
under, and breached, an affirmative
duty to warn the decedent of any

explicit
statements of
what defendant
wants from
court

potential hazard he might encounter
in the course of his haphazard rescue attempt. This court should
reject this contention, however,
because the facts of this case
simply do not support the proposi-
tion that the defendant owed the
decedent <u>any</u> duty whatsoever.

A. Duty Defined

In support of her theory of
recovery, plaintiff relies upon the
line of authority that holds the

direct quotation
of law

"owners and occupiers of land owe a
duty to firemen to warn them of
hidden perils, where the owner or
occupant knows of the peril and has
the opportunity to give warning of
it." <u>Clark v. Corby</u>, 75 Wisc. 2d
292, 295, 249 N.W.2d 567, 570
(1971). <u>See also</u> W. Prosser, <u>Law of
Torts</u> § 60 at 381 (4th ed. 1971).
This principal is generally regarded
as the majority view. <u>See generally</u>,
J.P. Ludington, Annotation, <u>Duty and
Liability of Owner or Occupant of
Premises to Fireman or Policeman
Coming Thereon in Discharge of His
Duty</u>, 86 A.L.R.2d 1205 (1971).

14

The Judiciary has developed a simple four-prong test to determine when the "duty to warn" requirement has accrued to a particular defendant. To trigger the requirement, each of the following four elements must be adequately demonstrated.

judicial interpretation

There must be: "(1) A hidden hazard--a concealed danger that foreseeably created an unreasonable risk to others; (2) which hidden hazard or danger is known to the landowner; (3) which hidden hazard or danger is not known <u>and not observable</u> by the fire fighter; and (4) existence of a <u>clear opportunity</u> for the landowner to give warning of the hidden hazard." (Emphasis supplied.) <u>Clark</u>, 249 N.W.2d at 570. <u>Cf. Romedy v. Johnston</u>, 193 So. 2d 487, 490 (Fla. Dist. Ct. App. 1967).

separate paragraph for the four prongs gives them additional emphasis, as does numbering them

[The syntax of this quoted sentence is rather clumsy: a good time to paraphrase]

B. Defendant Was Under No Duty to Warn Decedent of Potentially Hazardous Conditions

An application of the four-prong test to the facts of the present case demonstrates conclusively that defendant was under no duty to warn the decedent of the potential hazards surrounding the cliff area. While defendant contends that no evidence supports the existence of either of the first two "prongs" of the test, defendant will focus the

["application," a nominalization, weakens sentence]

application of law to facts

15

acknowledges all prongs but directs readers to third and fourth prong

court's attention on the overwhelming body of evidence that directly <u>negates</u> the existence of the third and fourth "prongs."

minor concession up front

Defendant concedes that the visibility in the area at the time of the rescue attempt was lessened by the onset of nightfall. While this fact standing alone might lend some support to plaintiff's contention that the drop-off was hidden from decedent's view, the events that transpired immediately after decedent's arrival on the scene substantially alter that view. The evidence is uncontroverted that, before embarking on their rescue mission, the decedent and his colleague lit the area they were to trek with the headlights of the rescue truck. Additionally, each of the men operated a flashlight to help choose his path over the rocky terrain. These lighting sources enabled the men to view each other at a distance of 150 feet. Under these conditions, the drop-off of the rock face would have been "observable" to all but the most careless of individuals. Defendant contends that he was under no duty to warn decedent of such an "open and obvious" danger. <u>Buren v. Midwest Indus.</u>, 380 S.W.2d 96, 99 (Ky. Ct. App. 1964). Accordingly, plaintiff's case fails under the third prong of the "duty to warn" test.

[transition "additionally" smoothes chronology into legal theory]

[transition "accordingly" creates causation]

16

Similarly, the fourth prong of the test also precludes recovery under the duty to warn theory. This is true because defendant never had a <u>clear</u> <u>opportunity</u> to warn the decedent of the potentially dangerous escarpment. The sworn depositions indicate that the defendant had suffered a serious fall that resulted in a severe fracture of his right leg, as well as various other abrasions and contusions. While he lay in agony at the foot of the rock face, defendant was apparently dazed and could do little more than attempt a feeble cry for help. Plaintiff must prove that despite this extremely helpless and confusing condition, defendant had the presence of mind to survey the area so that he might guide the decedent safely to the scene, but abstained from doing so out of simple negligence. No such proof is possible. The facts demonstrate conclusively that Wilson discovered the defendant in a "hysterical" state that would militate against his ability to warn the decedent of the nearby cliff. <u>Whitten v. Miami-Dade Water and Sewer Authority</u>, 357 So. 2d 430 (Fla. Dist. Ct. App. 1978).

The above analysis makes clear that defendant was under no duty to warn decedent of the existence of the escarpment. Because defendant cannot breach that which he does not owe, plaintiff should be barred from recovery under the "duty to warn" theory.

annotations:

reader may have forgotten fourth prong— be more explicit

[word choice similar to Statement of Facts: *severe fracture, agony, dazed*]

sentence length shifts here to very short and very effective

[word choice of "escarpment" implies only a fool would miss the edge of a cliff illuminated with shining headlights]

17

stronger
heading here

IV. INDEPENDENTLY, DECEDENT'S CONTRIBUTORY NEGLIGENCE BARS RECOVERY

A. The Contributory Negligence Doctrine

law

It is the duty of all persons to observe ordinary care for their own safety. Thus, if a plaintiff fails to discover or appreciate a risk that would be apparent to a reasonable man or intentionally exposes himself to a danger (of which he is aware), he is contributorily negligent as a matter of law. Prosser, <u>Handbook of the Law of Torts</u> § 65. Under common law negligence principles, the plaintiff's contributory negligence completely bars any recovery. Restatement (Second) of Torts § 446.

application of
precedent

This same principle applies to emergency rescue cases where a rescuer acts unreasonably or attempts to rescue in an unreasonable manner. <u>Kreiger v. Crowley</u>, 182 So. 2d 20 (Fla. 1965); <u>Wolfinger v. Shaw</u>, 292 N.W. 731 (Neb. 1940). The test of whether a rescuer's effort was so unreasonable as to preclude recovery is whether he acted with due regard for his own safety, or acted so "rashly or imprudently" as to bar recovery. <u>Altamuro</u>, 540 F. Supp. at 876; <u>Ryder Truck Rental, Inc. v. Korte</u>, 357 So. 2d 228, 230 (Fla. Dist. Ct. App. 1978); <u>Cords v. Anderson</u>, 259 N.W.2d 672, 674 (Wis. 1977). Other courts

18

There is also evidence from Wilson that Brennan was running over the rocks and continually slipping and falling. He was traveling so quickly, in fact, that he was approximately 150 feet in front of Wilson when he ran over the cliff. Brennan reasonably should have known that his conduct was imprudent--his slipping and falling could have injured an accident victim, and in fact did result in his own death. Further, Brennan had knowledge that he wore only leather-soled shoes, and that these shoes were not the proper shoes for running over mountains. If he was not aware of this fact before the rescue attempt, then he surely became aware of it as he traversed the rocks. As such, the contributory negligence bar applies to dangers of which he knew or should have known. <u>Barrett v. Robinson</u>, 65 F.R.D. 652, 658 (E.D. Pa. 1975); <u>Brant v. Van Zandt</u>, 77 So. 2d 858 (Fla. 1954).

Plaintiff's decedent also failed to keep a proper look-out in his hasty search for Brown. Although he had sufficient light from both the truck's headlights and his own flashlight, he was traveling so fast and paying so little attention to his surroundings, that he failed to observe the cliff's edge. If plaintiff contends that there was not enough light for the decedent to see the mountain's dangers, then decedent was still under a duty to proceed with caution under the

slanted language melds fact with slant: "reasonably should have known," "had knowledge that"]

application

"paying so little attention" anticipates plaintiff's responses to this argument

20

using similar formulations of this rule have barred recovery when the rescuer acts in a "rash or reckless" manner, <u>Solgaard v. Atkinson</u>, 491 P.2d 821, 825 (Cal. Ct. App. 1971), or fails to act "as a reasonably prudent man under the circumstances." <u>Kennedy</u>, 441 F.2d at 564; <u>Alford v. Blake</u>, 385 F.2d 1010, 1012 (5th Cir. 1967); <u>Baker v. Alt</u>, 132 N.W.2d 614, 615 (Mich. 1965). In all such cases, a rescuer bears a duty to act reasonably under the circumstances and failure to observe such a standard of conduct disentitles him to recovery.

additional precedent

[citations interrupt text]

effective conclusion

[two indepen-dent clauses need a comma]

B. Decedent's Carelessness Constitutes Contributory Negligence, Thus Barring Recovery

Plaintiff's decedent admitted his own negligent conduct when he yelled to Wilson to "watch out and try not to run on the rocks" because "it's too hard." This admission proves that Brennan knew and appreciated the dangers of the rough terrain and yet was unwilling to use the requisite caution demanded by the situation. Where rescuers fail to avoid "known perils," recovery under the Rescue Doctrine is barred. <u>Trowell v. United States</u>, 526 F. Supp. 1009, 1013 (N.D. Fla. 1981). Further, mere forgetfulness does not excuse the failure to avoid a known peril. Beebe v. Kaplan, 177 So. 2d 869 (Fla. Dist. Ct. App. 1965).

incorporation of record to establish fact

["this admission" slants]

law

19

"Darkness Rule." Darkness is, in itself, a warning to proceed either with extreme caution or not at all, and ordinarily a person who follows an unfamiliar course in the dark and sustains personal injuries is guilty of contributory negligence as a matter of law. <u>Barrett</u>, 65 F.R.D. 652; <u>Bredder v. Leidenfrost</u>, 134 F. Supp. 487 (N.D. Pa. 1955); <u>Bridges v. Hillman</u>, 82 N.W.2d 615 (Minn. 1957); <u>Wolfe v. Green Mears Constr. Co.</u>, 286 P.2d 433 (Cal. Dist. Ct. App. 1955).

authority

Finally, plaintiff's decedent was not justified in behaving recklessly, as he knew that the search and rescue team had been called and was on its way to find the accident. In fact, they arrived only minutes after plaintiff's decedent ran off the cliff. Thus, no evidence suggested a pressing emergency necessitating decedent's reckless conduct. Accordingly, the plaintiff should be denied recovery.

transition signals conclusion to follow

[is "team" singular or plural? inconsistent here]

[smooth argument of paragraph aided by transitions: *finally, in fact, thus, accordingly*]

V. CONCLUSION

As indicated above, defendant cannot be held liable for the injuries suffered by plaintiff for the following reasons: (1) decedent was acting in the capacity of a professional rescuer when he undertook the ill-fated rescue of defendant; (2) defendant owed decedent no duty to

paragraph restates argument in order of Statement of Facts and Table of Contents

warn of open and obvious dangers;
and (3) decedent's rash and imprudent conduct was the proximate cause
of his injuries. For these reasons,
defendant respectfully prays that
this court deny plaintiff recovery
in this matter.

22

APPENDIX III

Answers

POSSIBLE ANSWERS TO ADDITIONAL
EXERCISES, CHAPTER 1
(See page 24)

1. Only if readers already know both rules and can mentally contrast them will this paragraph work. Either a footnote detailing the two texts or a short comparison of the important language within both rules will allow readers to enter the world the writer has already studied.

2. Although it is fairly clear what the writer's point was, the paragraph jumped around a bit. I reordered the sentences so that the discussion of the case came first, followed by the application of the precedent to the clients' facts. Your answer may be quite different, and if so, you need to be able to articulate your decisions. As reorganized (with some minor editing), my paragraph now reads:

❶ In arguing our clients' case, it will be crucial that we prove the Trevors' use of the road is sufficiently analogous to <u>Perkins</u> so that the caveats of <u>Stone</u> should not apply; in this regard, several facts could redound to our benefit. ❹ In <u>Perkins</u>, the citizens of

Darlington County used the road to reach a sandy, beach-like area where they launched fishing boats and engaged in other recreational activities that could reasonably be construed as seasonal (i.e., summer) in nature. ❷ Similarly, while our clients used the road for only fifteen years, and only during the summer months, they did use it on a daily basis during those months. ❸ Thus, it is possible to infer that the character of the use in <u>Perkins</u> was the same as in our case. ❺ Moreover, the concentrated use of the road by the Trevors and their neighbors could be interpreted as being widespread—it almost certainly is more widespread than the use of the road described in <u>Stone</u>.

3. **Bloat's argument that the changes are insignificant is unconvincing for at least four reasons. First,** "[i]t does not lie with a defendant who has been so employed and for building it to say that his own performance would not be beneficial to the plaintiff." **American Standard** [cite]. In **American Standard**, the **court** was relying on <u>Chamberland v. Parker</u>, in which the plaintiff hired Parker to erect a monument that would reduce the value of his premises. [Cite.] **That court** held that a duly paid contractor could not decline to build it based on his belief that the monument would not be beneficial to the plaintiff. [Cite.] Similarly, Bloat, in the Babbitts' case, cannot justify nonperformance based on the fact that the higher cabinets and a platform stove may reduce the resale value of the house.

Next, the Babbitts' decision to move is immaterial to the expectation at the outset and throughout the work of the contract on their home. **Indeed,** it is likely that the Babbitts paid a higher contract price for the more expensive copper pipe and for the special construction involved in unusually high cabinets and a platform stove.

Third, the construction was completed in 1994. **Even if the** Babbitts could sell the house and move this month, more than a full year has passed during which the Babbitts have not been able to reap the benefits of the higher working surface that they paid for.

Finally, even if the decision to sell is factored into the significance of the breaches, their decision to add to the house may enhance the importance of full performance. **Although** copper pipe may not affect the market value of the house, it is a significant selling point for potential buyers.

4. Editing just the topic sentence improves the coherence of the paragraph and also provides a more effective transition from the thesis paragraph.

> **In determining whether or not a landowner has dedicated land to the public by implication, courts consider the length of time that the public has used the road; however, long use by the public alone does not establish implied dedication.** A similar case involved a road whose public nature was established by its use for fifty years. County of Darlington v. Perkins, 239 S.E.2d 69, 70 (S.C. 1977). The court in Darlington found that an easement had been acquired by implied dedication where as many as sixty-five people using a similar road for over fifty years did establish the road's public nature. Id. at 70. However, another case showed that public usage for fifty years is by no means enough in and of itself to infer an implied dedication. Stone v. International Paper Co., 359 S.E.2d 83, 85 (S.C. Ct. App. 1987). The court in Stone, upon determining that the volume of traffic was not great, did not find implied dedication even though the road had been used by the public for over fifty years. Id. at 84. This may be helpful to the Trevors' claim by showing that fifty years is simply an arbitrary number. Still, the number of years of public use is relevant and must be substantial. Whether or not fifteen years, as in the present claim, is sufficiently substantial is uncer-

tain, but nevertheless is well short of the length referred to in prior cases.

5. The paragraph is sufficient and offers a set-up. The headings follow the set-up. However, the topic sentences offer little insight into each section and could have been crafted with more specific detail.

6. The TWOC had some immediate success during the spring and summer of 1937. **By** August 1937, **for example**, the committee and ACWA had negotiated 29 agreements, covering 23,000 workers, 17,000 of whom were in the textile industry. Resistance to unionism stiffened during the winter, **however, and** in spite of some successes elsewhere the TWOC reported only about 25,000 workers under contract by the spring of 1938.

In addition to the usual employer opposition, the TWOC faced the beating and kidnapping of organizers, antiunion citizens' committees, the Ku Klux Klan, antiunion religious revivalists **and** the AFL. The AFL was offering itself to employers and workers as a more respectable alternative. **And** the TWOC campaign, **like** almost every effort to unionize the southern textile industry, was interrupted by a recession.

When the TWOC became the Textile Workers' Union of America-CIO in May 1939, it had 858 contracts covering 235,000 workers. A management evaluation in 1939 placed the TWOC's card-carrying membership in the south at about 20 per cent of the region's 350,000 cotton workers, **and** only 15 per cent paid dues regularly. The union was able to get contracts covering many fewer than this; **only** 5 per cent of the South's spindles were estimated to have been affected by union contracts, **and** a third of these were no longer in force by April 1939. An examination of TWUA records reveals an average of about 10,000 members in the south in 1939. The union encountered much more opposition in the south than in the north. **Though** the southern unions won more elections, the northern locals had many **more** closed shops, **more** active contracts, **and** fewer antiunion complaint cases filed with the NLRB. Herbert J. Lahne said:

> In the South, **by** the end of 1939, there were indications (such as a falling off in the number of NLRB elections held) **that** the union had reached the end of the more readily organizable sections of this traditionally difficult territory. . . . If the T.W.U.S. fails in the Southern cotton mills it cannot really succeed elsewhere.

Reorganization. **In** 1939, the AFL **re**constituted the UTW around several federal labor unions **and** some dissident groups from the CIO. Southerners were prominent in its **reor**ganization, **and** efforts to **reor**ganize the south played an important part in its plans.

POSSIBLE ANSWERS TO ADDITIONAL
EXERCISES, CHAPTER 2

I. Practice with Passives and Ambiguity (page 70)

1. Since a 28 U.S.C. § 1983 civil action **may entitle** defendant RAVENSWOOD to qualified immunity, **we must determine** whether defendant RAVENSWOOD's conduct violated any clearly established statutory or constitutional right.

2. **The defense was unable** to determine if the first **amendment protected** the conduct, and if, under the <u>Nearich</u> test, the allegations were insufficient.

II. Practice with Long Sentences (page 71)

Break into units.

1. In this connection, Plaintiff will show **(1)** that the **trucks'** design and manufacture of the brakes and brake adjusters were within the exclusive control of Defendants, **(2)** that Plaintiff had no means of **learning** the method or manner in which the product was designed and manufactured, and **(3)** that the product came into Plaintiff's possession in the same condition it was in when it left the **Defendants'** control. (*Or make separate sentences.*)

2. Defendants Rawdon Crawley, Pitt, and Sedley d/b/a Vanity Plaza Shopping Center **knew** that Plaintiff was using the common areas of the Vanity Plaza Shopping Center. **Defendants** intentionally and willfully entered into a contract for sale that interfered with the **Plaintiff's** lease **that required that** the Plaintiff's access rights to the common areas of the Vanity Plaza Shopping Center were protected. **Their deliberate sale**, therefore, **caused** the breach of Plaintiff's contract

with Defendants Sharp and Vexating Properties Investment, Inc.

OR

Defendants Rawdon Crawley, Pitt, and Sedley d/b/a Vanity Plaza Shopping Center intentionally and willfully entered into a contract for sale that interfered with the lease contract held by the Plaintiff. **They interfered knowingly,** because the Plaintiff was using the common areas of the Vanity Plaza Shopping Center and the Defendants did not reserve the Plaintiff's access rights to the common areas of the Vanity Plaza Shopping Center. **These rights** were protected under the contract and thus the Defendants breached the Plaintiff's contract with Defendants Sharp and Vexating Properties Investment, Inc.

Move the verbs.

1. However, this Court's **statement indicates** that **it considered** the Defendant's **Reply, which** contained the first fraud on the court argument. **The Court also had considered** the Defendant's assertions that "nothing could be further from the truth" and that Company's statements were "absolutely false."

OR

However, in the earlier order **the court stated that** it had received the Defendant's Reply, which contained the first fraud on the court argument. **That statement was** certainly indication that **the contents of the reply were** considered, and **thus** the Defendant's assertions that "nothing could be further from the truth" and that Company statements were "absolutely false" are sensational distortions at best.

2. Callins **asserted** two factors were against him in his motion for a new trial: **(1) that** jurors felt compelled to sentence him to death for the capital murder because they had not been aware during the first punishment hearing that they would also be sentencing him for capital murder, **and (2) that** they had assessed life imprisonment as punishment for the robberies.

OR

Callins **asserted (1) that the** jurors felt compelled to sentence him to death for the capital murder because they had not been aware during the first punishment hearing that they would also be sentencing him for capital murder, **and (2) that** they had assessed punishment for the robberies at life imprisonment. **These assertions were resolved** against him as a factual matter at the hearing on his motion for a new trial. *(Note that moving the subject close to the verb revealed a disagreement in number between the original "assertions" and "was.")*

Evaluate the length.

State Insurance Code Annotated Article 21.12 § 3(c) requires the State Treasurer to hold the deposit exclusively for the protection of any "customer" obtaining a final judgment against the corporate Local Recording Agent. **Section 3(c) also** allows the withdrawal of a "corporate Local Recording Agent financial responsibility deposit" only upon an affirmative showing **that (1)** it has withdrawn from business and has no unsecured liabilities outstanding, **or (2)** the corporation can prove financial responsibility by furnishing an errors and omission insurance policy or by posting a bond.

III. Practice Reorganizing Left-Handed Sentences (page 72)

Flip-flop or break.

1. **The court of appeals held** that mental distress was not a proper element for recovery in an action by a homeowner against a furnace seller who negligently installed the furnace resulting in a fire that destroyed the home and contents.

2. **This lease shall be void if** Landlord cannot obtain assurances satisfactory to Landlord that a separate rendition will not cause additional roll-back taxes on the **Landlord's** land adjacent to the Leased Premises, which is presently taxed on its agricultural value.

IV. Practice Placing Citations (page 73)

Make the text outweigh the citation.

1. An attorney cannot be held liable to third parties for acts committed within the scope of attorney-client relationship, absent fraud or negligence in the drafting of an estate planning document. Anderson v. McBurney, 467 N.W.2d 158, 160 (Wis. Ct. App. 1991); Brown v. LaChance, 477 N.W.2d 296, 300 (Wis. Ct. App. 1991). This exception has been narrowly construed by the courts of Wisconsin, which have held it valid in a limited context.

2. In an attempt to establish that commercial contracts can also be personal in nature, Plaintiffs misconstrue the holdings of Stewart v. Rudner, 84 N.W.2d 816 (Mich. 1957), Avery v. Arnold Home, Inc., 169 N.W.2d 135, 137 (Mich. Ct. App. 1969), and Allinger v. Kell, 302 N.W.2d 576, 581 (Mich. Ct. App. 1981).

OR

Plaintiffs misconstrue the holdings of three distinct and different cases in an attempt to establish that commercial contracts can also be personal in nature. <u>See</u> <u>Stewart v. Rudner</u>, 84 N.W.2d 816 (Mich. 1957), <u>Avery v. Arnold Home, Inc.</u>, 169 N.W.2d 135, 137 (Mich. Ct. App. 1969), and <u>Allinger v. Kell</u>, 302 N.W.2d 576, 581 (Mich. Ct. App. 1981).

V. Practice with Paraphrasing and Quoting (page 73)

1. *(first paragraph)* A quotation is not a topic sentence.

(second paragraph) There are no transitions to the block quotation defining intoxication.

(third paragraph) (a) No transition explains why readers next must understand "presumption." (b) No transition or explanation switches readers to *Reardon*.

2. Need a comma to introduce sentence quotation.

3. Direct quotation with changed capital/lowercase requires quotation marks, or sentence should be rewritten to become indirect quotation without bracketed changes.

VI. Practice Constructing Parallel Sentences (page 74)

Create parallel items.

1. Alternatively, plaintiff has not proved the necessary elements to prevail on the charge of intentional misrepresentation: (1) a material misrepresentation; (2) false material representation; (3) representation known by speaker to be false; (4) representation that the plaintiff was intended to rely on; (5) plaintiff's reliance on the misrepresentation; and (6) injury suffered by the plaintiff.

OR

Alternatively, plaintiff has not proved the necessary elements to prevail on the charge of intentional misrepresentation: (1) it must be a material misrepresentation; (2) the misrepresentation must be false; (3) the speaker must have known that it was false; (4) the statement must have been made with the intention that the plaintiff rely on it; (5) the plaintiff must have relied on the misrepresentation; and (6) the plaintiff must have suffered injury.

2. Other provisions of section 6 provide for the requisites of the application for a bondsman's license, for an investigation and hearing by the board, and **for** its denial of the application or approval conditioned on the applicant's filing of the required security deposits.

Tabulate this sentence to check parallelism.

3. If the list that follows the colon makes up an integral part of the introductory sentence, writers should remember: (1) to indent all of each item and to number each item, (2) to begin each item with a lowercase letter, (3) to end each item except the last with a semicolon, (4) to use a semicolon and "and" or "or" on the next-to-last item, and (5) to conclude the last item with a period unless the list does not conclude the sentence.

OR

If the list that follows the colon makes up an integral part of the introductory sentence, writers should remember:

(a) to indent all of each item and to number each item,
(b) to begin each item with a lowercase letter,
(c) to end each item except the last with a semicolon,
(d) to use a semicolon and "and" or "or" on the next-to-last item, and
(e) to conclude the last item with a period unless the list does not conclude the sentence.

POSSIBLE ANSWERS TO ADDITIONAL
EXERCISES, CHAPTER 3

I. Practice Finding Jargon (page 108)

1. This claim **contradicts** (**opposes**) one of the most deeply held beliefs of our society.

2. Manufacturing will have the final say in **extending the time frame**.

3. **Poor attendance has confused us, and we cannot** know the status of work items. Therefore, we cannot **meet** the schedule.

4. Thank you for **helping resolve** these issues.

II. Practice Finding Noun Strings (page 108)

1. other local-exchange companies' tariffs **for access service** for switched-transport per-minute rates

2. parent-company debt-service requirements

3. well established common-law cause of action (OR: well established, common law cause of action)

4. state jeopardy diesel-fuel tax assessments (OR: state-jeopardy)

5. the correct substantive-evidence rule test

6. six-inch thick concrete pallets (OR: six inch-thick concrete pallets)

7. certified-return-receipt postcard of plaintiff's motion (OR: certified-return postcard-receipt)

III. Practice Eliminating Wordiness (page 109)

1. profound

2. tuna

3. I believe (*or delete phrase*)

4. my unemployed wife

5. the first case filed

6. five state laws now

7. emergency

8. opinion

9. next

10. in the future (OR: soon)

Prepositions

1. This effort was made **casually**.

2. The grade was not the teaching **assistant's** choice.

Unnecessary words

1. The Company's **not purchasing** insurance breached the Dismantling Contract **by not complying** with Paragraph G. (OR: The Company's failure to purchase insurance breached the Dismantling Contract by failing to comply with Paragraph G's obligation.)

2. The Commission **concluded** that the plaintiff should not have been in court.

3. **This** brief **examines** the Equal Rights Amendment as a positive defense in an employment discrimination case.

4. *Correct.*

5. **The** earlier discussion of **time** computation is relevant here. However, **under** one statutory interpretation, the ninety-day period is computed from the original due date.

6. No definitive line of demarcation **determines** whether the proposed arrangement is a sale and leaseback or a financing arrangement for sales tax purposes.

IV. Practice Spotting Ambiguous Pronouns (page 110)
Ambiguous pronouns

1. The design of roads and bridges is a discretionary function, and the State will not be liable **for deciding the design. This lack of liability** is consistent with cases that hold decisions made at the policy level instead of operational level are immune.

2. Caldwell did not cross-examine Hapless in the presence of the jury and now contends, as he did on direct appeal, that by not being able to go into Hapless' background, he was prevented from showing **Hapless'** bias or prejudice for testifying as he did, in violation of **Hapless'** Sixth Amendment right to confrontation.

3. In <u>Veneer</u>, the alleged tort-feasor would have been at a tactical disadvantage if the lawsuit were delayed by the injured party. This **disadvantage** prompted the court to say that justice **should** permit a **timely continuance.**

4. The municipality would have the information concerning the location of the arrest and the identity of the co-defendant policeman in its possession; the defendant could easily combine the **location and identity** with the information contained in the complaint. The **combination of information** will probably provide a sufficiently specific factual basis for the time of the alleged violation, the place where it occurred, and those responsible.

5. The court in <u>Matthews</u> held that where "plain, adequate, and complete" relief is available, the aggrieved party "is left to that remedy in the state courts" unless a federal question is involved. 284 U.S. 526 (1927). Following the enactment of § 1341 in 1937, **this state-remedy theme** was broadened by the United States Supreme Court.

Placement of "only," "however," and other connecting adverbs

1. Success on the grounds of limitations can be had **only if** the court follows Wilson's lead and recognizes the appropriate statute of limitations is provided by the wrongful death statute.

2. In the event a lawsuit of either type could be successfully prosecuted, the courts would prohibit non pari-mutuel racing at the track **only until** registration can be completed.

3. First, the City asserts that a medical malpractice cause of action can be proven by the testimony of an outside medical expert **only**. The expert has, however, contradicted his own theory.

4. He wants to file in state court. However, it has only been two weeks since the case was dismissed from the federal court. (*acceptable as written, or "two weeks only since"*)

5. Agent further acknowledges that Owner will accept financing of the sale through **only one** of the four following methods.

POSSIBLE ANSWERS TO ADDITIONAL
EXERCISES, CHAPTER 4

Practice with Punctuation (page 134)

Proper punctuation

1. Mr. Brown also claims that during the arrest Officer Smith became "highly abusive," denied Mr. Brown his right to speak, and struck the plaintiff twice without provocation, causing him bodily injury.

2. In the decision in <u>Santex,</u> supra, the court also held that the employee need prove only that filing the claim was a reason for termination, not the sole reason. *(or a dash)*

3. Plaintiff further argued that the statute did not apply because the unit was only a component part of a larger whole, thus not by itself an "improvement." *(or you can leave both commas around "by itself")*

4. The Texas Supreme Court has stated that, generally, common law indemnity is grounded in either (1) different qualities of negligence, (2) a breach of duty between tortfeasors, or (3) vicarious liability. <u>Bonniwell v. Beech Aircraft Corp.,</u> 663 S.W.2d 816, 823 (Tex. 1984).

5. The common law doctrine of negligence consists of three essential elements: a legal duty owed by one person to another, a breach of that duty, and damages proximately caused by that breach. <u>See Rosas v. Buddy's Food Store,</u> 518 S.W.2d 534, 536 (Tex. 1975). *(or keep dash)*

6. The second issue of first impression is whether the reservation of the power to prosecute, compromise and settle, or otherwise deal with any claim for additional royalties is illegal and void as an attempt to engage in the unauthorized practice of law.

7. A statement apparently made to the EEOC by Weeks shows that Weeks spends only 50% of his time developing new business, **whereas** Johnson spent all of his time developing new business. (Document Response No. 6). Weeks also states that when he began his employment at the Bank, he assumed 1/3 of Johnson's loans **while** Bowers and Ehrenpreis evenly split the remaining loans.

8. The decisions, holding that a creditor of the promise can maintain action on the contract of which he is the beneficiary, have been based upon no one well-defined theory. (*original version also acceptable*)

9. Likewise, Oxy's and Mobil's attempt to invoke the inherent jurisdiction of the District Court (pursuant to Article 5, section 8 of the Texas Constitution, sections 24.007, 24.008 and 24.011 of the Texas Government Code, and section 85.241 of the Texas Natural Resources Code) is not proper.

OR

(*divide into two sentences*) Likewise, Oxy's and Mobil's attempt to invoke the inherent jurisdiction of the District Court is not proper. See Article 5, section 8 of the Texas Constitution, sections 24.007, 24.008 and 24.011 of the Texas Government Code, and section 85.241 of the Texas Natural Resources Code.

10. Such participation, he claims, was fundamentally unfair.

11. The Comptroller's audit assessment was correct because the seven (7) customer contracts stated material and equipment, labor, and sales tax as separated amounts, making these seven (7) contracts separated contracts under Section 151.056.

12. Defendants committed to provide 370 psychiatric acute-care beds in facilities that conform to the new standards.

13. In addition, this group was charged with developing proposals by which the state-funded health-education institutions could assist or augment TDC.

(1) Which is the most matter-of-fact? (2) Which allows a longer pause and perhaps greater emphasis on "his best friend"? (3) Which creates the longest pause? (4) Which has a formal, almost solemn quality?

1. matter-of-fact: *A*

2. long pause and emphasis: *B and C. C emphasizes the "friend."*

3. longest pause: *C*

4. formal: *C or B*

Annotated Bibliography

To find answers to style and usage questions, I always reach for the grand old standbys: easy-to-use style books that answer my questions succinctly. Here are my favorites:

C. Edward Goode, *Mightier Than the Sword: Powerful Writing in the Legal Profession.* Blue Jeans Press, 1989. Goode quickly teaches readers the elements of English grammar and then manipulates those elements to prove his 19 "Rules of Good Writing." His intelligent, flowing ideas can help improve anyone's style. After 200 easy-to-read pages about legal style, he wades bravely into the content of memoranda, offering specific advice for organization, quotations, and even *The Bluebook*—all made concrete by referring to a mini-casebook he has compiled and a memorandum he includes. The book is full of humor ("Be fair and nonsexist, but don't be stupid"), personal asides, and strong prose.

Joseph Williams, *Style: Lessons in Clarity and Grace.* Scott, Foresman, and Company, 1981. Williams' well-written book emphasizes manipulating sentence order and structure. Style, he proselytizes, "should not be something that boxes you in, but a means to free your intellect and imagination from the obscurity that confused prose puts between you and your ideas." This book isn't specifically directed at legal writers, but all of us can learn from unusual chapters on "Controlling Sprawl" and "A Touch of Class." Interestingly, he divides grammar into "rules and RULES": real rules (only seven of them), nonrules (e.g., "never begin a sentence with 'because'"), optional rules (e.g., split infinitives, prepositions ending sentences), and special formality (ways to elevate your style).

Tom Goldstein and Jethro Lieberman, *The Lawyer's Guide to Writing Well.* McGraw-Hill, 1989. A lawyer and a journalist teamed up to offer realistic advice to legal writing dilemmas. "The Mechanics of Getting It Down" and a honest look at writer's block are followed by techniques for anticipating readers' needs: "Writing the Lead." An especially useful section on organization ("By the Way, I Forgot to Mention . . .") begins with a typical fact situation and the four paragraphs of a resulting brief; afterwards, the authors analyze the paragraphs' logic, topic sentences, and flow. The later editing chapters are divided into fixing problems and creating powerful sentences: The examples are excellent and memorable ("Referring to *Roe v. Wade,* a student wrote: 'Scientists do not yet know whether life begins at contraception.' The student didn't mean to be funny, but like many an unwary writer, he was oblivious to the meaning of certain words.").

Hollis Hurd, *Writing for Lawyers.* Journal Broadcasting & Communications, 1990. Intended for paralegals and new law clerks, this book hits the ground running and takes readers right along! First, Hurd defines a legal audience: people with too little time to read anything. Then he analyzes a legal audience's priority and logic system and uses that psychology as a foundation for his practical advice on general style, writing briefs, writing facts, and drafting. His real-life examples will catch your attention and stay with you long after you've put the book down. Each chapter contains numbered topic sentences in boldface type that allow a skimmer to retain most of Hurd's advice, and each subsequent discussion gives lively reasoning for that advice.

Richard Wydick, *Plain English for Lawyers*. Carolina Academic Press, 3d ed., 1994. Wydick's down-and-dirty advice can be read on the run: avoid multiple negatives, do not use lawyerisms, avoid cosmic detachment. Clear layout and sharp typography team up for one-page descriptions of common prose problems. A great feature of this book is the concluding exercises in each section—with answers in the back.

Texas Law Review Manual on Style. 8th ed., 1992. For the most conservative opinion about the exalted style of law reviews, I appreciate this little manual: Its Table of Contents and Index lead me to a law review editor's answers—quickly.

Theodore Bernstein, *The Careful Writer*. Atheneum, 1965. S.I. Hayakawa, *Choose the Right Word*. Harper & Row, 1968. These two alphabetized collections of words can hone your vocabulary with their discussions of synonyms and usage. I keep both on my shelf and refer to them regularly.

Ruggero J. Aldisert, *Logic for Lawyers*. Clark Boardman, 1989. This book isn't about style but rather about legal reasoning. After a few teaching chapters (inductive and deductive reasoning, Socratic method, common law paradigm), Judge Aldisert identifies logical fallacies and evaluates troublesome judicial opinions and their faulty reasoning. This book can help you understand and articulate your own organization—and perhaps teach you how to point out your opponents' errors.

Index